STACEY ANNE BATERI[

PHILIPPINE!

Copyright © 2017
by Stacey Anne Baterina Salinas and Klytie Xu

ISBN 978-1-947766-02-0

All rights reserved.

Printed in the United States of America.

No part of this book may be reproduced in any manner
whatsoever without written permission
except in the case of brief quotations
embodied in critical articles and reviews.

For information, address
*Pacific Atrocities Education, 730 Commercial Street,
San Francisco, CA 94108*

Stacey Anne Baterina Salinas
& Klytie Xu

PHILIPPINES' RESISTANCE

THE LAST ALLIED STRONGHOLD IN THE PACIFIC

Stacey Anne Baterina Salinas is an history PhD student currently attending the University of California, Davis. She received her Bachelor's degree from the University of California, Irvine and received her Master's degree from California Polytechnic State University, San Luis Obispo, both in American History. Her research focus is on Asian American History centering on the roles of Asian American women and their impact on America's Civil Rights Movement(s) and contributions to the diversity of the American woman's experience. She dedicates her late nights of research and writing to the many men and women who fought for her grandparents' and parents' native homes in the Philippines. Her maternal grandfather served as a Filipino USAFFE soldier, drafted from Baguio City, who survived the Bataan Death March. Along with her paternal grandmother's late night tales of her terrifying confrontations with the Japanese as a young girl in the northern provinces of Luzon, their histories of World War II serve as proof of the impacts and legacies of Asian America. Their stories and perseverance helped fuel both her desires and pursuit in writing histories on the humble heroes and innocents unable to voice their struggles and wisdom.

Klytie Xu is an undergraduate student attending the University of California, Santa Cruz studying Literature. Throughout her high school education, she noticed the lack of lesson plans and information regarding minorities' contributions to American and world history, which has driven her writing and research of this book. Klytie dedicates this book to those who served and those who lived to tell the story, including her own family. She hopes this book will inspire and teach others about the lesser known histories of sacrifice and determination.

Contents

Introduction 7

CHAPTER 1
The Japanese Invasion &
Conquest of the Philippines 11

CHAPTER 2
The Formation of the Underground
Philippine Resistance 29

CHAPTER 3
The Makeup of the Guerrilla Forces:
Ethnic, Political, & Social Diversity of a Common Cause 47

CHAPTER 4
Bataan Death March 87

CHAPTER 5
The Female Faces of the Philippine Guerrillas 101

CHAPTER 6
The Liberation of the Philippines 127

CHAPTER 7
The Legacy of the Philippines and
Its Peoples' Roles in World War II 141

Epilogue 157
Resources 161

Timeline

- **1930s:** General Douglas MacArthur organizes military units for the Pacific region in the Philippines
- **December 7th, 1941**: Japanese Attack on Pearl Harbor
- **December 8th, 1941:** Japanese Attack on Clark Field
- **May 5th-6th, 1942:** Japanese Attack on Corregidor
- **April 9th, 1942:** Bataan Death March
- **January 2nd, 1942:** Japanese occupy Manila and declare it an open city
- **January 1942:** Filipina guerrilla Yay Panlilio broadcasts her first acts of televised resistance via radio station in Manila
- **1942:** Wendell Fertig's Filipino Christian and Moro guerrilla establishment begins taking shape on Mindanao
- **1942:** Young Philippine Military Cadets establish the guerrilla organization, the Hunters ROTC
- **March 29th, 1942:** Philippine Communist and Socialist leaders meet to establish the Hukbalahap (Huks) to fend off the Japanese and all forms of imperialism in the Philippines
- **December 16th, 1944:** Liberation of Mindoro and other Mindanao regions by Moro guerrilla units
- **October 20th, 1944:** Return of General MacArthur to the island of Leyte
- **October 26th, 1944-December 1944:** The U.S. Navy defeat the Japanese in the Battle of Leyte Gulf
- **February 4th, 1945:** The Retaking of Manila by the Allied Forces and Guerrillas
- **August 15th, 1945:** The Japanese Imperial Army officially surrender in Baguio City, Philippines
- **September 2nd, 1945:** Official liberation of the Philippines from the Japanese
- **July 4th, 1946:** Philippines celebrate their official independence

INTRODUCTION

The beautiful archipelago of the Philippine Islands consists of over 7000 islands in the Pacific. The country hosts a variety of geographical landscapes ranging from lowland provinces, mountainous regions, jungle, and rainforests. The Philippines' natural landscapes, harbors, and resources represented opportunities for trade and conquest.

Chinese privateers, Malaysian ethnic groups, Negrito peoples, and Polynesian are just a few of the groups, emerging out of Taiwan as early as 4000 BCE, who traveled to and established communities throughout the Philippine Islands.[1] Just as the Philippine geographic landscapes are diverse, so are the ethnic and language groups that comprise the people there. The culmination of such a variety of language groups and ethnic peoples and their networks of trade and communication throughout the islands produced an amalgamation of syncretic cultures, languages, ideologies, and peoples. Despite the common association that islands are isolated bodies of geopolitical influences, the legacy of these various groups and their constant interactions throughout East Asia, South

---

[1] Yves Boquet, *The Philippine Archipelago* (Dijon: Springer, 2017) 24-28.

Asia, the South Pacific, and Southeast Asia remain a part of the heritage of religions, languages, and culture that is still prominent there today.

The imperial and colonial history of the Philippines spans nearly four hundred years and is just as unique and filled with various characters, politics, and agendas. Within that history alone, the Philippine peoples have experienced multiple wars for the control and sovereignty of the Philippine Islands. The aftermath of the Spanish American War during the early twentieth century would represent another era that would prove the inexhaustible morale of Filipinos to gain their right to govern themselves. The Philippine American War would last nearly ten years. Guerrilla rebel soldiers made up of a range of Filipino citizenry throughout the islands would put up a hellish fight towards independence but unfortunately would succumb to the firepower of the United States. American policies during the war would include tactics similar to America's treatment and disregard of the Native American communities throughout the nineteenth century.[2] America's most recent wars, the Korean War, the Vietnam War, and the wars in the Middle East, saw terrible repercussions for civilians sympathetic towards sovereignty, Philippine civilians were no exception. These acts of coercion and imperialist domination included waterboarding, the exiling and execution of rebel leaders, unjust destruction of villages and barrios, the spreading of prejudiced propaganda both domestically and internationally promoting the ethnic peoples as bellicose and savage, and unnamed incidents of ruthless assaults on innocent bystanders including women and children.[3] The American imperialist policies under President William McKinley and Theodore Roosevelt would re-

---

[2] Greg Nickles, *Philippines-The Culture* (New York: Crabtree Publishing Company, 2002), 28-35.

[3] David Silbey, *A War of Frontier and Empire: The Philippine-American War, 1899-1902* (New York: Macmillan, 2008), 12, 62, 91.

sult in the establishment of a military and political American presence. Similar to the influence of Spanish culture, American culture would make a profound impact on the Philippine culture throughout much of the Philippine islands. This form of acculturation and rule would set the precedent for a long political and economic relationship between the Philippines and the United States well into the twenty first century, nearly seventy five years after the Philippines celebrated its independence in 1946.[4] The Philippines' resilience and honor in preserving their country and cultures would be proven in one of their most desperate situations; the Japanese invasion of the Philippine Islands in December of 1941.

One of the Philippines' most noted contributions to global affairs is their courageous efforts in the liberation of the Philippines in the Pacific Theater of World War II. Civilians, soldiers, villagers, and Philippine men and women from all walks of life, contributed to the lesser known grassroots underground resistance after General MacArthur's departure in 1942 to Australia. Without direct help or contact from the Allied forces, the Philippine citizenry were left with little means for surviving the imperial Japanese assault upon their homelands. The Philippine countrymen could choose to either stage a resistance to the Japanese Imperial Army or aim for a passive stance in order to avoid armed violent repercussions.[5] Many brave Filipinos and Filipinas, as guerrillas, chose to defend their communities, islands, cultures, and sovereignty from a new imperial presence. With the surrender of Japanese forces in the fall of 1945, the guerrilla sacrifices proved fruitful, promising a brighter future for a new nation in the Pacific. Their experiences and contributions to the liberation of the Philippines continue to represent the ba-

---

[4] Huping Ling & Allan W. Austin, *Asian American History and Culture: An Encyclopedia, Volume 1 & 2* (New York: Routledge, 2015), 81, 256, 257.

[5] Frances B. Cogan, *Capture: The Japanese Internment of American Civilians in the Philippines, 1941-1945* (Athens: University of Georgia Press, 2000), 76,103, 110, 121, 179.

sis that allowed for the establishment of the Philippines as a free and democratic nation state.

CHAPTER 1
The Japanese Invasion & Conquest of the Philippines

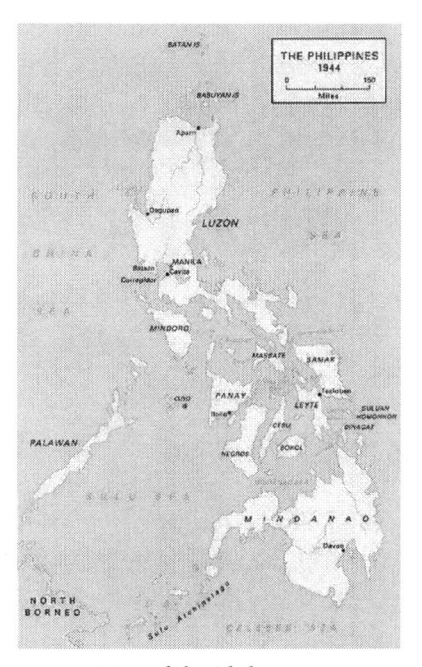

Map of the Philippines

The geographic locations of the many different islands and regions of the Philippines in context to one another is crucial in order to comprehend the course of war and the Japanese and American strategies of attack. [6]

---

[6] "Leyte," *U.S. Army Center of Military History*, Last Modified October 3 2003,

Leading up to invasion

Although the Japanese attack on Pearl Harbor in December of 1941 is widely known as the beginning spark of the Pacific War, conflict between the Japanese Imperial Army and Western powers began as early as the 1930s, due to the Western countries' disapproval of the recent Japanese conquests in China and Indochina in addition to Japan's increasing militarism. By July of 1940, the United States enforced an embargo on its export of oil, steel, and iron to Japan and freezed Japanese assets in America, consequently greatly impacting the Japanese economy as well as the demand for supplies to continue Japanese military efforts.[7] Between the possibility of economic decline or withdrawal from war, the Japanese were further encouraged to begin expanding their campaign in Southeast and East Asia, which included the occupation of the Philippine Islands. This would prevent American forces from utilizing the Philippine Islands as an operational base and would place the Japanese in a strategic position to seize much needed natural resources in the Dutch East Indies and Malaya.[8] By early December of 1941, Japanese forces were positioned on the island of Formosa (present-day Taiwan), waiting to carry out their battle plan.

The United States recognized theses growing tensions, prompting American preparation for the likelihood of war as it continued to occupy the Philippine Islands. After the establishment of the Philippine Commonwealth[9], President

---

Last Accessed August 2, 2017, http://www.history.army.mil/brochures/leyte/leyte.htm

[7] Clayton Chun. *The Fall of the Philippines 1941-1942* (Great Britain: Osprey Publishing, 2012), 6-7.

[8] Louis Morton. *The Fall of the Philippines*. Vol. 2. (Office of the Chief of Military History, Department of the Army, 1953), 52.

[9] Under the Tydings-McDuffie Act, the Philippine Commonwealth was established for a ten year transitional period before the Philippines would be granted full independence.

Quezon enlisted the help of General Douglas MacArthur[10], recalled from retirement, who had the executive ability and experience to command the defense of the archipelago and strengthen the newly formed Philippine Army of the Commonwealth.[11] The Philippine defense became organized into the unified force of the US Army Forces in the Far East (USAFFE) consisting of the Philippine Army, the Philippine Constabulary, the Philippine Scouts, and the US Army's Philippine Department. The US Army had 22,532 personnel stationed in the Philippines during this time, about half were Philippine Scouts, whom were well trained.[12] The United States Asiatic Fleet supplied additional naval support for the USAFFE.[13] Throughout MacArthur's preparation for war, he began to assemble FEAF, the Far East Air Forces, hoping American air power would become a deterrent to Japanese forces. Maj. Gen. Jonathan M. Wainwright assumed command of Northern Luzon forces and led the Philippine Division, the largest unit within the U.S. Army in the Philippines.[14] Over 250,000 Filipinos enlisted to defend their homeland, being promised American citizenship, full veteran benefits, and equal pay.[15] However, training proved to be a difficult task. As Japanese attack became more imminent, divisions were not fully organized or completely trained. Obstacles included the language barriers both between Americans and Filipinos and among Filipinos themselves, because of the several different dialects the Filipinos spoke. Furthermore, MacArthur had trouble receiving adequate financial aid and equipment. The shortages of clothing, personal hygiene

---

[10] Chief of Staff of the US Army during the 1930s and World War I.
[11] Morton, *The Fall of the Philippines*, 9.
[12] Clayton Chun. *The Fall of the Philippines 1941-1942*, 16.
[13] Louis Morton. *The Fall of the Philippines*. Vol. 2., 45.
[14] Morton, *The Fall of the Philippines*, 21.
[15] Ashley N. McCall-Washington, "Surrender at Bataan Led to One of the Worst Atrocities in Modern Warfare," USO, Last Modified November 14th, 2015, Last Accessed August 3rd, 2017, https://www.uso.org/stories/122-surrender-at-bataan-led-to-one-of-the-worst-atrocities-in-modern-warfare

supplies, and weaponry impacted the necessary training. By December of 1941, the estimated strength of the Philippine Army was approximately 120,000 men.[16] General MacArthur believed he still had time to continue training and establish the appropriate beach defenses, assuming Japanese attack would not occur until April of 1942.[17]

Philippine Scouts train with antitank guns at Fort McKinley.[18]

---

[16] Chun, *The Fall of the Philippines 1941-1942*, 19.
[17] Chun, *The Fall of the Philippines 1941-1942*, 32.
[18] U.S. Army Center of Military History, Last Modified July 9 2006, Last Accessed August 3 2017. http://www.history.army.mil/books/wwii/5-2/5-2_2.htm

Philippine Scouts are shown building a bridge at Fort McKinley, the headquarters of the Philippine Army. [19]

Initial Japanese Invasion

Only hours after the attack on Pearl Harbor, Japanese naval and air forces began to simultaneously launch surprise strikes across Southeast Asian countries, including the Philippines.[20] The fall of Pearl Harbor eliminated any American plans to come to the assistance of American-occupied Philippines, leaving the country in isolation. The Japanese planned for a quick conquest of the Philippines within fifty days.[21] General MacArthur was notified of the Pearl Harbor attack and ordered to execute the planned war strategy, Rainbow 5 War Plan. Thinking it was defeatist,[22] MacArthur had previously changed the long-established plan of War Plan Orange (WPO) developed before World War I, favoring a more active defense; fighting the Japanese on the beachheads, rather than a withdrawal into Bataan. There is question concerning whether or not Japanese invasion of the

---

[19] Morton, *The Fall of the Philippines*, 18.
[20] Morton, *The Fall of the Philippines*, 84.
[21] Michael Norman and Elizabeth M. Norman, *Tears in the Darkness: The Story of the Bataan Death March and its Aftermath* (New York: Farrar, Straus, and Giroux, 2009), 56.
[22] Chun, *The Fall of the Philippines 1941-1942*, 32.

Philippines would have been prevented if MacArthur had allowed senior commander, General Brereton, to launch a raid on Japanese occupied Formosa, where Japanese bombers were delayed due to foggy weather.[23] Furthermore, if MacArthur had accepted WPO and instead focused on fortifying Bataan, this could have prevented the many American and Filipino casualties on the Philippine beaches. Nevertheless, the Japanese forces were so overwhelming, it may not have prevented the eventual defeat of the Philippines.

On December 8th, 1941, approximately 17 hours after Pearl Harbor, led by Japanese Lt. General Masaharu Homma, Japanese air forces began bombing Clark Field, a major American air base on the island of Luzon. Hangars, barracks, and warehouses were completely ruined as casualties increased. The American forces present were helpless in defense of the air base because most of the B-17 bombers and P-40 fighters were parked to refuel and therefore vulnerable to attack.[24] As Japanese bombs rained on Clark Field, Japanese planes simultaneously attacked the base at Iba, also located on the island of Luzon. The initial Japanese aerial attacks resembled Pearl Harbor, as the Japanese successfully caught American forces by surprise, establishing Japanese air superiority. With the American air strength nearly wiped out, the Far East Air Force (FEAF) was destroyed as an "effective fighting force" after only one day.[25] Half of American bombers were destroyed, although Filipino and American pilots attempted bravely to challenge their enemy. One such Filipino pilot was Capt. Jesus Villamor, assigned to the Philippine Army Air Corps alongside the FEAF. He was later awarded for his extraordinary heroism in aerial combat while piloting a P-26 fighter on December 10, 1941. Two days later, he would lead six pursuit planes after 54 Japanese bombers. Villamor would

---

[23] Chun, *The Fall of the Philippines 1941-1942*, 34, 35.
[24] Chun, *The Fall of the Philippines 1941-1942*, 39.
[25] Morton, *The Fall of the Philippines*, 88.

also coordinate guerrilla efforts in Luzon, Mindanao, and the Visayas under MacArthur's orders.[26] [27]

Jesus Villamor, gets out of his plane. For his heroic actions and fighting efforts during the initial Japanese aerial attacks, Villamor was awarded the Air Force's Medal of Valor.[28]

Following Japanese aerial bombardment in various other locations including Nichols Field, the Del Carmen Field, Nielson Fields, and the Cavite naval base, an attack on the Japanese Formosa was no longer possible without the necessary American supplies and power. The few remaining flyable B-17s escaped by December 17th, further weakening American and

---

[26] "Valor Medals for Jesus A. Villamor," *Hall of Valor,* Last Accessed August 3rd, 2017. http://valor.militarytimes.com/recipient.php?recipientid=6215

[27] "Jesus Villamor: Soldier, Spy," *Filipinas Heritage Library,* Last Accessed August 3rd, 2017. http://www.filipinaslibrary.org.ph/filipiniana-library/filipiniana/70-features/267-jesus-villamor

[28] Farm Security Administration, *Jesus A. Villamor.* March 1, 1943. Farm Security Administration/Office of War Information Black and White Negatives,Library of Congress. https://en.wikipedia.org/wiki/Jes%C3%BAs_A._Villamor#/media/File:Jesus_A._Villamor.jpg

Filipino forces.[29] This beginning catastrophe foreshadowed the following Japanese conquest of the Philippine islands.

Japanese attack on Cavite Naval Base, shortly after the Pearl Harbor attack.[30]

The same day Japanese air forces took off to destroy American air bases, the Japanese sent three land invasion forces to begin sailing south from Formosa, planning a total of six landings pushing towards Manila.[31] General Wainwright was responsible for defending Northern Luzon with his troops, but many of the Filipino fighters were still not fully trained or adequately equipped with weapons by the time of war.[32] During the Japanese Lingayen Gulf landings, American and Filipino forces were able to rely on the Philippine Army divisions to defend their land with the Filipinos' knowledge of the area, despite lacking in weaponry like tanks and armored cars.[33] Filipino and American defenses used 30- and .50-cal machine guns along their beach defenses causing heavy Japanese casualties. Despite the small strength of the Japanese landing troops, the poorly trained Filipino soldiers along with the Asiatic Fleet's submarines, and the small number of air fighters were unable to hold off battle-hardened Japanese

---

[29] Chun, *The Fall of the Philippines 1941-1942*, 42.
[30] Morton, *The Fall of the Philippines*, 93.
[31] Morton, *The Fall of Philippines*, 98.
[32] Chun, *The Fall of the Philippines 1941-1942*, 43.
[33] Chun, *The Fall of the Philippines 1941-1942*, 44.

forces. Many Filipino units fled upon encountering the Japanese.[34] As a result, MacArthur failed to stop Japanese forces from advancing towards Manila and the retreat south to Bataan Peninsula became inevitable. Continuing defeats of various Luzon fronts including a Japanese landing on Lamon Bay, only 60 miles from Manila, finally persuaded General MacArthur to retreat. After declaring Manila an open city on December 26, 1941, MacArthur evacuated to the island of Corregidor to evade Japanese capture.

During the American and Filipino retreat, Philippine Army engineers worked alongside Americans to build obstacles meant to slow down the Japanese invaders. This allowed additional time for troops and supplies to withdraw.[35] Since the Lingayen Gulf and Lamon Bay landings, MacArthur had lost 13,000 men, while Homma lost 2,000 men.[36]

The First Battle of Bataan

Japanese tanks advance in Bataan, where Americans and Filipinos engage in a fierce battle.[37]

---

[34] Chun, *The Fall of the Philippines 1941-1942*, 46.
[35] Chun, *The Fall of the Philippines 1941-1942*, 53.
[36] Chun, *The Fall of the Philippines 1941-1942*, 57.
[37] Kent G. Budge, "Philippine Islands," *The Pacific War Online Wikipedia*, Last Modified 2013, Last Accessed August 4, 2017. http://pwencycl.kgbudge.com/

By January of 1942, the Japanese Imperial Army had conquered most of Southeast Asia, and the Philippine island of Corregidor and the Bataan Peninsula remained the last Allied strongholds on the Pacific front. With the American troops retreated into Bataan, a harsh reality settled: there was limited supplies of food, medicine, and weapons and the original WPO (War Plan Orange) planners' assumption of a rescue by the Pacific Fleet in six months was no longer possible.[38] With the responsibility of 80,000 American and Filipino soldiers who were already retreating, the army did not expect to take on responsibility for the additional 26,000 civilians and refugees in Bataan, and were forced to half ration the food supply.[39]

To defend Bataan, MacArthur took advantage of naturally rugged geographic features to establish areas of defense against advancing Japanese troops. From his position in Corregidor, MacArthur continually assured his American and Filipino troops that help was arriving, but in actuality, this was an empty promise.[40] The Japanese did the unexpected and conquered the rough terrain MacArthur's defenses had relied upon. Despite fierce counter attacks from Filipino units defending the Abucay defensive line, MacArthur ordered their retreat. The Japanese repeated this feat at the Mauban defensive line, and after surrounding a few Filipino units, the Filipino troops were forced to retreat once again.[41] In a change of strategy, Homma ordered the Japanese landing of troops behind the Bagac-Orion line, engaging the American and Filipino units for days. However, the Japanese failed to defend their territory resulting in a minor Allied victory.

P/h/Philippine_Islands.htm
[38] Chun, *The Fall of the Philippines 1941-1942*, 57.
[39] Chun, *The Fall of the Philippines 1941-1942*, 57.
[40] Chun, *The Fall of the Philippines 1941-1942*, 63.
[41] Chun, *The Fall of the Philippines 1941-1942*, 61.

By mid-February, the Japanese suffered about 2,275 casualties and unable to break the Bataan defense, Homma decided to wait for reinforcements.[42]

One of the last stands along these defensive lines was made by Capt. Jose Tando, one of the finest Filipino Constabulary officers. During the Battle of the Points, he crept towards the enemy and personally took out an enemy machine gun with a hand grenade hit. Tando would later be awarded for his personal bravery. [43]

Sgt. Jose Calugas was another soldier of the many Filipinos who valiantly fought in the Battle of Bataan. As a Philippine Scout, he was assigned to assist the Filipino and American troops in withdrawing. When Calugas' area came under attack, he courageously ran across 1,000 yards under enemy fire to put a machine gun that had fallen from Japanese fire back into action and fired successfully at the enemy. Singlehandedly manning the gun, Calugas was able to stop 60 advancing Japanese vehicles. For his bravery, Calugas was the first Filipino to be awarded the Congressional Medal of Honor, the highest American military award.[44]

---

[42] Chun, *The Fall of the Philippines 1941-1942*, 66.
[43] Donald J. Young, *The Battle of Bataan: A Complete History*, 2d ed. (McFarland & Company, 2009), 122.
[44] Jose Calugas Jr., "Jose C. Calugas Sr.", *US-Japan Dialogue on POWs*, Last Accessed August 3rd 2017. http://www.us-japandialogueonpows.org/Calugas.htm http://www.historylink.org/File/10939

Sgt. Jose Calugas' contribution to the fierce Battle of Bataan is representative of the many persistent and brave Filipino and American soldiers who continued to resist despite intense Japanese attack and Allied shortages.[45]

After months of fighting in Bataan, American and Filipino troops were incredibly weakened. Japanese forces blocked any supplies or reinforcements from reaching the hungry, tired, and sickened troops. Malaria, beri-beri, and dysentery ravaged the men, more than half of the remaining soldiers were no longer considered "combat-effective".[46] The promised reinforcements and supplies never came, as the Allied powers prioritized the operations in the European theater over the Philippines. Seeing the inevitable loss of the Philippine fight, MacArthur was ordered to leave Corregidor, making Wainwright the commander of the Luzon forces. Wainwright was instructed by MacArthur to fight until the end without a surrender in mind. In turn, Wainwright named Maj. Gen. Edward King as the commander of the forces on Luzon, while he was promoted as the new commander of all the US

---

[45] US Signal Corps, "Jose Calugas, Medal of Honor," *National Archives,* Last Modified April 12 1945, Last Accessed August 2, 2017. https://commons.wikimedia.org/wiki/File:Jose_Calugas_Medal_of_Honor_(cropped).jpg

[46] Ashley N. McCall-Washington, "Surrender at Bataan Led to One of the Worst Atrocities in Modern Warfare".

forces in the Philippines. On March 12th, 1942, MacArthur evacuated to Australia vowing to return.

In April of 1942, the Japanese launched a final attack on the Allied defense line. The remaining American and Filipino forces were forced to withdraw and retreat after a series of heavy air and artillery attacks. With additional reinforcements, Homma and his troops were finally able to break the last defensive Bagac-Orion Line, against the crumbling but still fighting American and Filipino troops. Seeing his weakened and starved men no longer capable of holding onto their defenses and operate as a coordinated unit, field commander, General King, made the decision to surrender more than 70,000 Filipino and American troops at Bataan on April 9, 1942, the largest surrender in American military history. Approximately, 63,000 Filipino troops and 12,000 American troops became prisoners of war.[47] A few soldiers escaped to join the local Filipino guerrilla forces, refusing to become Japanese captives.

The desperate fight against the Japanese reached an end with the surrender of General King, who accepted sole responsibility of his decision.[48]

---

[47] Ashley N. McCall-Washington, "Surrender at Bataan Led to One of the Worst Atrocities in Modern Warfare".
[48] U.S. Army Center of Military History, "Surrender", Last Modified June 1 2006, Last Accessed July 31, 2017. http://www.history.army.mil/books/wwii/5-2/5-

Japanese soldiers guard the Filipino and American prisoners of war. The large unexpected number of captives after the Battle of Bataan created a logistical chaos.[49]

The Battle of Corregidor

After the fall of Bataan, the island of Corregidor remained the final obstacle to Japanese victory in the Pacific theater. Without Corregidor, the Japanese would not have full access of Manila Bay, a valuable natural harbor. Japanese forces began aerial bombardment from the end of December to April of 1942, as the United States Army, Navy, and local Filipino soldiers continued to resist. The defenders of the island lived under the Malinta tunnel. Although safe from enemy assault, they were living in miserable conditions with low rations, many suffering from disease. Men became increasingly weak as a result of poor nutrition and their physical ability to fight dwindled. Japanese bombing allowed little food supply to reach the island. Led by Major General Kureo Taniguchi, Japanese forces landed on the island of Corregidor on May 5, 1942. Under heavy fire, General Jonathan Wainwright sur-

---

2_26.htm
[49] Morton, *The Fall of the Philippines*, 462.

rendered Corregidor by the afternoon of the next day, May 6, 1942. The defeat of Corregidor signified the fall of not only the Philippines but the rest of Asia. 600-800 Americans and Filipinos died during the final assault on Corregidor.[50] The captured American and Filipino prisoners of war were marched through Manila before arriving to Bilibid Prison and then distributed to various prisoner camps.

General Homma did not miss an opportunity to conquer the southern Philippines during the Battle of Bataan and Corregidor, where the main targets were the Panay and Cebu islands. Americans and Filipinos tried to delay the Japanese by destroying bridges and roads, still the city of Cebu fell by early April and Panay by April 20th of 1942. On the island of Mindanao, the American and Filipino forces were defeated by May 9th. The Mindanao-Visayan forces commanded by Brigadier General William Sharp, was told not to surrender by MacArthur, despite Wainwright's orders. Several American officers agreed with the senior General and escaped with their troops to the jungles to join pockets of guerrilla resistance. However by June 9th of 1942, six months after the beginning of Japanese conquest, all organized resistance ended.[51]

---

[50] Chun, *The Fall of the Philippines 1941-1942*, 81.
[51] Chun, *The Fall of the Philippines 1941-1942*, 81, 84, 85.

Taken on May 3, 1942, only a few days before Wainwright's surrender at Corregidor. The American and Filipino men were located into this tunnel to safeguard from attack.[52]

American soldiers exit Malinta tunnel and surrender at Corregidor.
[53]

---

[52] Morton, *The Fall of the Philippines*, 532.
[53] National Archives, "Surrender of American troops at Corregidor, Philippine

Although the American and Filipino troops had surrendered, the Japanese time schedule was disrupted by the unexpected lasting defense from the Americans and Filipinos. General Homma had hoped to end his campaign in 45 days within his 50 day timeline. However, due to the courageous efforts of the Filipino and American men who fought for sixth months, the swift conquest of the Philippines the Japanese had hoped for did not occur. This resistance delayed the greater Japanese plan in controlling the Pacific and would continue on until MacArthur's return, as the Filipino and American guerrillas' continued to resist during Japanese occupation. When researching the Filipino involvement during the decisive and heroic battles of Bataan and Corregidor, it is difficult to discover particular cases of Filipino bravery, and their contributions are often overshadowed by American experiences, even though the majority of the fighting force were Filipino.

Later American troops would partner with Filipino guerrillas in camaraderie against the Japanese.[54]

Islands," Last Modified May 1942, accessed August 2, 2017. https://catalog.archives.gov/id/535553.

[54] U.S. Army Center of Military History, "Special Operations in the Pacific", page 77.

CHAPTER 2
The Formation of the Underground Philippine Resistance

The near simultaneous attack on the Philippine Islands and the attack on Pearl Harbor were part of the Japanese military strategy of gaining control of the Pacific whilst eliminating any standing presence of the American military.[55]

---

[55] J.P. Wegley, "Mobilizing for WWII: Timeline," *In History*, Last Accessed July 9th, 2017, https://www.timetoast.com/timelines/mobilizing-for-wwll.

The surrender of Bataan marked the struggles to come for the Philippine Islands and its people.[56]

After the Allies' surrender of the island of Corregidor, the main military defense of the Manila Bay, radio connection and communications stopped as the Japanese military continued their invasion of the Philippine Islands. Despite this cut in communication, pockets of American and Filipino soldiers were able to escape the Death March of Bataan and evade the radar of the Japanese military. Filipino soldiers who escaped from Bataan and other POW camps went into the mountains of Luzon or relied on Filipino locals to guide them to other safe zones harboring guerrilla fighters or Allied stragglers.[57] One such Filipino soldier who was able to escape after the fall of Corregidor was Ramon Magsaysay Sr. He would become a major face of the Western Luzon Guerrilla Force commanding over 10,000 guerrillas and would later become the seventh president of the Republic of the Philippines.[58] Other soldiers, similarly to Magsaysay, would form

---

[56] World War II Foundation, "Film Details Local War Hero's Exploits," *World War II Foundation*, Last Modified 2017, Last Accessed July 7th, 2017, http://www.wwiifoundation.org/2015/09/13/film-details-local-war-heros-exploits/.

[57] Stephen L. Moore, *As Good As Dead: The True Story of Eleven POWs Who Escaped from Palawan Island* (New York:Penguin, 2016), 144.

[58] Napolean D. Valeriano & Charles T. Bohannan, *Counter-Guerrilla Opera-*

resistance groups, join other Filipino led guerrilla units, or go into hiding with the help of Filipino civilians. Many made desperate attempts to establish contact with MacArthur and the American Intelligence Bureau of the South Pacific, risking their lives to cross the coasts into open ocean to connect with Allied Intelligence.[59]

American and Filipino soldiers put a great deal of labor in establishing and maintaining radio communication and supply networks with American and Australian Allies during the Japanese occupation of the Philippine Islands from 1941-1945. MacArthur and his general staff believed that morale for the Allies had to be fueled in order for both civilians and surviving Filipino and American soldiers to stage a substantial defense against the Japanese.[60] In order to achieve a foundation of morale, securing a network of underground resistance groups became a major priority of General MacArthur and Pacific Naval Fleet admiral, Chester W. Nimitz. A survey of the terrain of the Philippine Islands, the locations of Japanese military centers, and the locations of the various anti-Japanese Filipino and Chinese guerrilla units, all had to be confirmed in order for the remaining Allied forces in the Pacific to have a chance of taking the Philippines out of enemy hands.

Several bands of resistance fighters sprouted up throughout the Philippine landscape. These groups had differing opinions as how to approach the Japanese occupation. Their nationalistic goals often drove the leaders of these groups to compete with one another on their political and regional agendas. One example of a politically driven resistance group

---

tions: *The Philippine Experience* (Westport:Greenwood Publishing Group ABC-CLIO: 2006), 67, 78, 80-88, 103.

[59] David W. Hogan Jr., *US Army Special Operations in World War II* (Washington D.C.: Center of Military History Department of the Army, 2014), 76, 81-88, 103.

[60] Ernesto Lee, *World War II Philippines: A Boy's Tale of Survival* (Xlibris, 2010), 12-14.

are the Hukbalahap Guerrillas. Originally a socialist organization composed of Filipino citizens, including peasant farmers, workers' unions, communist party members, and both urban and rural laborers, all Huk supporters shared common interests in an independent Philippines prior to World War II. The Huk, like many other nationalist political organizations, found their agendas further fueled by another imposing imperial force that threatened Philippine sovereignty.

Other military and political leaders like governor Confesor Tomas of the Philippine Island, Panay, also reinforced a long held nationalist and democratic rhetoric as Japanese forces encroached upon the Philippine Islands. As the war time governor of the Free Panay, Tomas continued to write and orate his beliefs that a free democratic Philippines would need to overthrow the presence of the imperial Japanese, declaring their role in the Pacific as more menacing and detrimental than that of either the Spanish or American imperial legacy.[61] The amalgamation of nationalist rhetoric, the visible string of atrocities including brutal warfare, raping, and killing of civilians seen throughout Manila, the barrios, and provinces served as a foundation for fueling the Philippine underground resistance.

Violent Breaches in the Conduct of War

Filipino communities prior to the Japanese occupation were already weary and concerned about the Japanese Imperial presence. News of their invasions on mainland China, the atrocities committed in Nanking in 1937, the harsh treatment of Koreans throughout the late nineteenth and early twentieth centuries as Imperial Japan began to expand

---

[61] Sven Matthiessen. *Japanese Pan-Asianism and the Philippines from the Late Nineteenth*
Century to the End of World War II: Going to the Philippines Is like Coming Home?
(Brill,
2016), 212.

throughout the Pacific, all served as markers of Japanese aggression in the Pacific. Although there were some Filipinos who believed that the Japanese Imperial Army represented an opportunity to liberate the Philippines from Western Imperialism, the violent breaches in the Japanese military conduct of war convinced the majority of Filipinos to side with the underground guerrilla movement.

The maltreatment of the Philippine civilians, how the Japanese Imperial Army torched the cultural and historical landscape of the Philippines, and the poor treatment of the Allied POWs, would culminate in fueling the fervor for the guerrillas to sacrifice their lives to end the Japanese atrocities in the Pacific.

The treatment of Filipino and American soldiers during and after the Bataan Death March represents just one of the many gruesome atrocities and breaches as to the proper conduct of war. The Bataan Death March stretching nearly 70 miles over the span of several days, was rife with Japanese soldiers maliciously harassing and killing both American and Filipino POWs that had surrendered at Corregidor and Bataan. Oral histories and memoirs of the survivors and the Filipino civilians, as recollected in the previous chapter, point to the visible brutalities that the Japanese Imperial Army utilized in their attempt at claiming the Pacific Theater. With scenes of bayoneted defenseless soldiers, public executions of Allied soldiers, and the deprivations to the Allied POWS of the prisoner camps, any form of friendly relations that the Japanese Imperial Army hoped to establish became highly suspect among the Philippine peoples.[62] Even Filipino civilians were beaten if they tried to provide water and sustenance to the marching soldiers. The intolerable Japanese actions during the Bataan Death March of April 1942 would

---

[62] Thelma B. Kintanar & Clemen C. Aquino, Patricia B. Arinto, Ma. Luisa T. Camagay, *Kuwentong Bayan/Noong Panahoon: Everyday Life in a Time of War* (Quezon City: University of the Philippines Press, 2006), 226-228.

foreshadow the future waves of physical and psychological mistreatments against the people of the Philippine islands. The March and its aftermath would fuel just one of the many sparks of Filipino grassroots sentiments for the total resistance of Japan's Imperial Army in the Philippines. These gruesome horrors of war instilled pockets of Allied POWS who were able to escape the March and POW camps on foot to lead or join fellow Filipino resistance fighters throughout Luzon.[63]

World War II American Anti-Japan propaganda noting the brutality of the Bataan Death March.[64]

---

[63] Hampton Sides, *Ghost Soldiers: The Epic Account of World War II's Greatest Rescue Mission* (Anchor Books, 2002), 91-105.

[64] Office for Emergency Management, Office of War Information, Domestic

Other instances of unjust brutalities enacted by the Japanese Imperial Army include the Palawan Massacre of 1944. American POWs in the Philippines were often rounded up and forced to do grueling manual labor. The POWs located near the city Puerto Princesa, on the island of Palawan, received inadequate medical attention, suffered starvation, and were forced to do labor intensive tasks like restructuring or fixing landing strips, trenches, or maintaining camp structures.[65] As the Japanese military began to realize the tide of war shifting to the the benefit of the Allied forces in both the Pacific and European Theaters, the call to exterminate any Allied survivors within Japanese hands became heavily considered as a last act of defiance and retaliation.[66] The remaining POWs of the camp were ordered into trenches, locked up, and burned. The Japanese military's extreme measures were meant to prevent the POWs from being rescued and eliminate any evidence of the camp, which culminated in the systematic murders known as the Palawan Massacre.[67] The trenches were set fire to, those American POWs who escaped were tracked, shot down, and burned. Only 11 of the 300 POW American soldiers stationed at Palawan survived.

Other American POWs who did escape were found and aided by local Filipino guerrillas who fed, clothed, hid, and provided networks of communication for the POWs to other American allies directly in contact with MacArthur or the guerrilla underground resistance. Historian Hampton Sides in his book, *Ghost Soldiers,* further emphasizes the impact

---

Operations Branch, Bureau of Special Services, "World War II Propaganda Poster," *National Archives & Records Administration*, [Public domain], via Wikimedia Commons, Last Modified January 28th, 2010, Last Accessed July 30th, 2017, https://commons.wikimedia.org/wiki/File%3AAnti-Japan2.png.

[65] Hampton Sides, *Ghost Soldiers: The Epic Account of World War II's Greatest Rescue Mission* (Anchor Books, 2002), 9-17.
[66] Sides, *Ghost Soldiers*, 22, 95, 212, 213.
[67] Sides, *Ghost Soldiers*, 13, 90, 129.

the survivors of the Palawan Massacre, like Eugene Nielsen, had in retelling their harrowing experiences as POWs to his guerrilla rescuers. American guerrilla leaders like Robert Lapham took the POW experiences of abuse and torture as reasons to further support military campaigns to raid civilian and POW camps before the Japanese forces could exact the same atrocities seen at Palawan elsewhere.[68] The overall roles of resistance that the POWs across Luzon took on heavily emphasizes how such Japanese breaches in the conduct of war in treatment of their POWs directly sustained the build up of the Philippine guerrilla resistance.

Filipino and American soldiers who survived both the Palawan Massacre and the Bataan Death March were not the only witnesses to the Japanese cruelties and breaches in the traditional conduct and treatment of POWs during wartime. Filipino civilians were both witnesses and victims themselves of the same brutalities enacted on the Allied soldiers throughout the war. Horror stories of the brutal war torn landscape of China during the initial stages of the Japanese invasion in the late 1930s had reached Philippine shores and newspapers. After the fall of Bataan and Corregidor, Philippine peoples too feared that the incidents of rape, bayoneting of infants and elderly, the ultimate leveling of cities, and the Japanese takeover of the natural resources and food stuffs would also play out on Philippine soil as the Japanese takeovers had demonstrated in China, Korea, and other parts of Southeast Asia. To the horror of the Philippine peoples, the waves of Japanese control would indeed enact such barbarities onto the Philippine Islands.

---

[68] Sides, *Ghost Soldiers*, 21.

As documented by survivor testimonies, Filipino and American soldiers were forced by Japanese officers to dig their own graves in the forms of trenches where they would be beheaded and buried. Depicted is a Japanese beheading party in one of the provinces of Luzon.[69]

The cruel actions (torture, kidnapping, murder, rape, extortion, unlawful arrests, censorship) of the Japanese secret military police, the Kempeitai, would encourage many Filipinos and Filipinas to continue to raise arms against the Japanese invaders.[70] Civilians out past the assigned town's curfew would face arrest by Japanese officers. Women would be selected by Japanese officers and relocated to serve as comfort women, a euphemistic term for sex slaves, never to be heard from by their families again.[71] As suspicions of the growing guerrilla underground resistance increased within the first two years of the Japanese takeover of Manila, the Kempeitai

---

[69] Battling Bastards of Bataan, "The Sack of Manila," *The Battling Bastards of Bataan Newsletter*, Last Accessed July 30th, 2017, http://www.battlingbastardsbataan.com/som.htm.

[70] Sven Matthiessen, *Japanese Pan-Asianism and the Philippines from the Late Nineteenth Century to the End of World War II: Going to the Philippines is like Coming Home?* (Brill, 2015), 174-177.

[71] Wallace Edwards, *Comfort Women: A History of Japanese Forced Prostitution During the Second World War* (Absolute Crime, 2013), Kindle, Introduction.

efforts of executing and jailing any civilians attributed with holding guerrilla or American sympathies also rose.[72] The unlawful jurisdiction of a foreign presence combined with daily intimidating confrontations and ultimatums set by the Japanese military heartened Filipino attempts to not only liberate their country but also secure networks of communication to re-establish an alliance with the USAFFE (United States Armed Forces of the Far East) and heads of the Pacific fronts; General MacArthur and Admiral Chester Nimitz.

During the sacking of Manila from February to March of 1945, the remaining Japanese and Korean officers left to defend the city looted and attacked block by block the streets of Manila, leaving in their path raped and murdered women and children.[73]

The visible signs of mistreatment, murder, rape, and destruction to the cultural and natural landscape of the Philip-

---

[72] Raymond Lamont-Brown, *Kempeitai: Japan's Dreaded Military Police* (Sutton, 1998), 52, 144, 146.

[73] Department of Defense, Department of the Army, Fort Leavenworth, Kansas, *Japanese Atrocities, Philippines, China, Burma, Japan*, National Archives Catalog, National Archives Identifier 292598, September 18th, 1947. Last Modified June 2007, Last Accessed July 30th, 2017, https://commons.wikimedia.org/wiki/File:FilipinoChildrenWW2.gif, https://catalog.archives.gov/id/292598.

pines further provoked civilians to form their local pockets of resistance. To prevent their families, homes, governments, and cultures from being uprooted entirely, Filipino insurgents, despite their pre-war contentions in relation to political parties, class, religion, and ethnic marginalization, found common ground in banding together to retake the Philippines.

Japanese Efforts to Cut Pathways of Resistance

As an imperial entity, Japan understood that the location of Philippine insurgent groups represented threats to their prominence in the Pacific and ability to control the Philippines. Without the total sentiment and acknowledgement of the Filipino people as to the leadership of the Japanese imperialist state, sentiments towards the Allies would continue to upset the power balance and attempts at the pan Asian coalition the Japanese government sought. Thus the risks that the Filipino Resistance fighters faced were both intimidating, frightening, and almost certainly meant the ultimate sacrifice of their lives and those that were associated with them. American soldiers, sympathizers to the Allied front, anyone who questioned the purpose of the Japanese occupation were known to be tortured, exiled, publicly executed, murdered along with their families, or forced into labor, internment, or prisoner of war camps (i.e. Baguio Internment Camp, Camp Holmes, Los Banos to name a few). Despite these frightful Japanese repercussions, Filipino morale would continue to grow after the Bataan Death March and military settlements of Japanese forces throughout Luzon.

The Japanese military believed that all ties to the Allies had to be cut off psychologically and culturally. Leaflets were made that described the Japanese military and empire as a friend and brother to the Filipino people and that together, they could form a Greater Asia.[74] Control over the Philippines' outlets of media became a major aspect of the Japanese military to infiltrate and eliminate any American and allied sympathies. Films produced by the Japanese Navy and the Japanese Propaganda Corps served as wartime propaganda that portrayed the Japanese occupation as positive and liberating for the Filipino people. These films were narrated in Tagalog, and declared that the Japanese had defeated the Americans, blatantly stating therefore that all Filipinos should cooperate and accept that the Japanese presence would become an essential aspect of their "liberated" country.[75]

The goals of the Japanese military in these films were to promote themselves as the benevolent protectors of the Filipino people. The films portray the Japanese officers as purveyors of goodwill who offer food, medical aid, and friendship. In return, the Japanese Propaganda Corps believed films like *Dawn for Freedom* (1944) would help to end Filipino sympathies and alliances with any western ideologies and therefore, eliminate any civilian attempts at aiding the survival of any straggler American military personnel or guerrilla fighters.

> Propaganda Short Films Produced by the Japanese Navy:
> https://www.youtube.com/watch?v=2bTEf1N_ij8
> https://www.youtube.com/watch?v=HkpaGj8rbcE

---

[74] Sven Matthiessen, *Japanese Pan-Asianism and the Philippines from the Late Nineteenth Century to the End of World War II: Going to the Philippines Is like Coming Home?* (Brill, 2016), 115-118.

[75] Matthiessen, *Japanese Pan-Asianism and the Philippines from the Late Nineteenth Century to the End of World War II*, 116, 117.

Japanese propaganda poster meant to persuade the Filipino peoples that the Imperial Japanese forces would help establish Filipino Independence from western influences.[76]

---

[76] SGM Herbert A. Friedman, "Japanese PSYOP During WWII," *Psywarrior*, Last Modified November 1st, 2003, Last Accessed July 9th, 2017, http://www.psywarrior.com/JapanPSYOPWW2.html.

Dawn of Freedom was a film part of the Japanese propaganda efforts to ameliorate the tensions between the Japanese military presence and the Filipino civilians, 1944.[77]

---

[77] Video 48. (2011). The war years (1942-45): Part two/ propaganda movies. Retrieved September 1, 2012 from http://video48.blogspot.com/2011/03/war-years-1942-45-part-two-propaganda.html.

The Japanese propaganda film, "Dawn of Freedom," portrayed the Japanese soldiers as comrades to Filipino civilians, whereas the Filipino insurgents and guerrillas were depicted as self serving, violent, soldiers who were preventing the Philippines' independence.[78]

Other means of gaining the trust of the Philippine peoples was through ideological and cultural mediums. The rules of warfare were not followed along all lines of the Japanese military that invaded the Philippine Islands. The news of executions, mistreatment of insurgents and Allied soldiers, the burning of cities and barrios, the rape of women and children were overwhelming and could not be left to only rumor. To silence any hostilities or revenge that the Philippine peoples might harbor, Japanese Catholic leaders at the beginning

---

[78] Pinoy Kollektor, "Dawn of Freedom - Philippine World War II Japanese Propaganda Film," *Pinoy Kollektor*, Last Modified October 12th, 2011, Last Accessed July 8th, 2017, http://pinoykollektor.blogspot.com/2011/10/48-dawn-of-freedom-philippine-wwii.html.

of the invasion of the Philippines were sent to the islands to ameliorate any tensions felt amongst the Filipino citizenry.

Members of the Japanese clergy did believe that their efforts in the Philippines was primarily to uplift, educate, and provide food and shelter to the Filipino people. Men like Father Gregory Shogi Tsukamoto served as a non-combatant in a Catholic Unit known as the Religious Section, a branch of the Japanese Propaganda Corps. The mission of the Catholic Japanese officers was to protect the the infrastructure of the Filipino Catholic churches and offer goodwill to the occupied islands.[79] The Religious Section's goals included protecting the wellbeing of the churches, schools, and hospitals which all served as cultural centers for the Filipinos the Japanese sought to occupy.

Despite this branch's efforts, Filipino, American, and European clergy were not spared and became one of the many casualties of the Japanese invasion. Many nuns and fathers lost their lives due to the bombing raids that littered the Philippine landscape. Others died by executions or were imprisoned in POW and civilian internment camps. Filipino Church records declare that nearly 300 clergy (nuns, fathers, deacons, bishops, etc.) died at the hands of the Japanese military.[80] These brutalities committed against both the Church and their neighboring communities led clergymen and women to also resist the Japanese Imperial Army. Many surviving clergy also served as guerrillas for the underground Filipino resistance in Northern Luzon like the famous Episcopal priest, Al Griffiths.[81]

---

[79] UCA News, "Japanese Priest Who Worked in the Philippines During War Honored," *UCA News: Asia's Most Trusted Catholic News Source*, Last Modified March 9th, 1993, Last Accessed July 6th, 2017, http://www.ucanews.com/story-archive/?post_name=/1993/03/09/japanese-priest-who-worked-in-philippines-during-war-honored&post_id=42928.

[80] Ernie A. De Pedro, "Plaza Dilao in History," *Lord Takayama Jubilee Foundation*, Last Accessed July 6th, 2017, https://takayamaukon.com/plaza-dilao-in-history/.

[81] North Lincoln County Historical Museum, "Historical Book Talk," *Best

Memoirs written and preserved by Griffiths' son, anthropology scholar Stephen Griffiths, are crucial examples that reveal that the grassroots movement against the Japanese occupation had encouraged all citizens from every walk of life, religious sect, socio-economic class and caste, to unite and retake the Philippines despite their low chances of success. These freedom fighters throughout the Philippines would make up the guerrilla combatants and reconnaissance agents that would allow for the the Allied forces to retake the Philippine Islands efficiently during the final stretch of the war.

Things Oregon: American Towns Media, Last Modified March 25th, 2017, Last Accessed August 3rd, 2017, https://bestthingsor.com/event/historical-book-talk-2017-03-25-lincoln-city-or.html.

CHAPTER 3
The Makeup of the Guerrilla Forces: Ethnic, Political, & Social Diversity of a Common Cause

The exiled Philippines' government, the Philippine Commonwealth Government, wanted to keep the morale of the Filipino and Filipino Americans high despite the high death tolls of civilians and soldiers throughout the islands. Artist and Filipino immigrant Manuel Ray Isip painted this poster in New York, drawing on art styles of Holly-

wood films and newspaper illustrations. The poster depicts a Filipino soldier hurling a grenade at the enemy while standing defiantly for the freedom of the Philippines. This poster was smuggled into the Philippine Islands and was circulated by the various guerrilla units beginning in 1943.[82]

The various insurgent groups recognized by General MacArthur's Intelligence Bureau consisting of specifically guerrilla units, were organized to represent military districts that in total amounted to ten recognized regional districts. The ten military districts in turn would manage and oversee the operations and reconnaissance of their defined areas. These regional districts would then report back to their allies in the Pacific (Australia and New Guinea) by making contact along the coasts often meeting up with Allied forces by radio communication or by the use of small makeshift boats and rafts that would reconvene with Allied submarines.[83]

Not all guerrilla units served directly alongside with the Allies. Many sought independently to protect and retake their native homes from the Japanese without the assistance of western militaries. Other guerrilla units would not be officially housed under the ten military districts that were recognized by MacArthur and the USAFFE (United States Army Forces of the Far East). Unfortunately, the efforts of all the Filipino guerrillas would continue to be either overshadowed, or unrecognized, because of the more popular and better preserved accounts of the non-guerrilla all American forces that would aid in the more prominent battles like the Liberation of Manila in 1945. Key American figures like General MacArthur (Supreme Allied Commander of the South West Pacific Theater) or Admiral Chester Nimitz (Leader of

---

[82] Manuel Ray Isip, "The Fighting Filipinos: Poster Story," *Filipino Executive Council of Greater Philadelphia*, Last Accessed July 8th, 2017, https://pinoyphilly.com/from-our-editors/the-fighting-filipinos-poster-story/.

[83] John D. Lukacs, *Escape from Davao: The Forgotten Story of the Most daring Prison Break of the Pacific War* (New York: Nal Caliber Penguin Group, 2010), 272.

Pacific Ocean Theater) continue to be showcased as the central guiding forces towards the liberation of the Philippines and Pacific overall. The focus on such well known leaders has unfortunately sidestepped the contribution of ethnic minorities, women, and ordinary civilians who participated in resisting the Japanese occupation throughout Southeast and East Asia.

The Many Faces of the Grassroots Resistance and Its Struggles Towards Unification

Contracts, collaborative agreements, and consistent strategic partnerships would not always be made between the many guerrilla units that arose during the course of the war. Furthermore, guerrilla units and other bands would differ in size, political party liaisons, their alliance with the Allied forces, and their overall means of resources, supplies, and military strategery.[84] Many of these groups were independent of one another and relied heavily on their respective local villages, or barrios, to make ends meet with artillery, clothing, housing, food, and what monetary means they could find.

Throughout the war effort, resistance organizations lacked proper supply networks and direct correspondence with American and Australian allies in the Pacific. Nonetheless, the guerrillas made efficient use of what supplies were available. Guerrilla soldiers distilled alcohol to make fuel, used metal from various items (curtain rods, metal from wrecked naval ships, etc.), and relied often on both rafts and traditional small fishing boats, bancas, to meet American submarines and naval crews for follow up reconnaissance.[85]

---

[84] Napoleon D. Valeriano & Charles T. Bohannan, *Counter-Guerrilla Operations: The Philippine Experience* (Westport: Praeger Security International, 2006), 7-9.

[85] Supreme Commander of the Allied Powers, General Staff of General MacArthur, *Reports of General MacArthur: The Campaigns of MacArthur in the Pacific, Vol. I.* (Library of Congress, 1966), 80-81.

The Filipino ethnic guerrillas made efficient use of the harsh jungle terrain and created clever booby traps (i.e. digging and making spiked pits throughout the jungle landscape) and placed homemade bombs (made from firecrackers and Japanese mines) throughout the dense jungles. These tactics and advantages of the rough natural terrain made it nearly impossible for the Japanese Imperial Army to infiltrate the dense Philippine jungles.

The guerrillas recruits, despite their tenacity and resourcefulness, were nonetheless limited by their poor networks of military, food, and medical resources. Many fighters succumbed to malaria, infection, malnourishment, and the harsh environment.[86] The earlier phase of the resistance paints Filipino guerrilla fighters often without proper military shoes or were without shoes entirely. Not all were armed with proper firearms. Some only held firearm relics from World War or had simple pistols, while others only had bolos (Traditional Philippine long knives similar to a machete for cutting sugarcane and used for combat).[87] This limitation ultimately led the scattered guerrillas to rely moreso on their fellow countrymen and women, often recruiting them into their forces similar to the guerrilla resistance staged during the Philippine American War.[88] This underground grassroots movement against the Japanese occupation continued to rely on everyday men and women to form the foundation of the guerrilla units that would help the Allied forces liberate the internment POW camps, entire Philippine Islands, and eventually push the last of the Japanese Imperial Army into the mountainous region of Luzon leading to the ultimate surren-

---

[86] Bernard Norling, *The Intrepid Guerrillas of Northern Luzon* (Lexington: University Press of Kentucky, 2005), 138.

[87] Norling, *The Intrepid Guerrillas of Northern Luzon*, 108, 190, 230.

[88] Renato Constantino & Letizia R. Constantino, *A History of the Philippines* (New York: Monthly Review Press-New York University Press, 1975), 262.

der of General Yamashita Tomoyuki and Admiral Denshichi Okochi on September 3rd, 1945.[89]

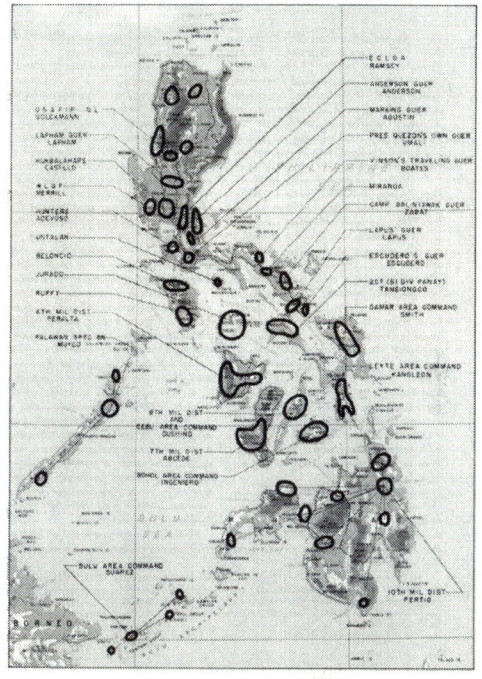

The Major Guerrilla forces recognized by General MacArthur and his staff labeled by their assigned military district and district leader.[90]

The Hukbalahap (Huks)

The Filipino Communist Party would play a major role in the underground resistance throughout the war. The founders and party members of both the Socialist and Philippine

---

[89] John Kennedy Ohl, *Minutemen: The Military Career of Robert S. Beightler* (Boulder: Lynne Reinner Publishers, 2001), 1, 225.
[90] Supreme Commander of the Allied Powers General Staff of General MacArthur, *Reports of*
General MacArthur: The Campaigns of MacArthur in the Pacific, Vol. I (Library of Congress, 1966), 299. Last Accessed July 8th, 2017, http://www.history.army.mil/books/wwii/MacArthur%20Reports/MacArthur%20V1/ch10.htm.

Communist Party throughout the 1930s, prior to the Japanese occupation, served as active nationalists and revolutionaries who sought an independent communist Philippine state. The leader of the Philippines first official communist organization, the Worker's Party, was Crisanto Evangelista.[91] It wouldn't be until after the Japanese capture and executions of Evangelista and his head deputy, Abad Santos, that Evangelista's communist and socialist guerrillas would come to call themselves officially the Hukbalahap in 1942. Their group's name, Hukbalahap, essentially translates to "people who are against the Japanese" or " the people's army against the Japanese" and would heavily resonate with local Filipino communities who experienced the daily abuse of the Japanese military presence.[92]

The Huk's main center of communication was on the island of Luzon in the swamp and dense jungle regions near Mount Arayat. Initially, Evangelista's forces were low on resources in regards to men, trained soldiers, weaponry, foodstuffs, and basic necessities like clothing. The Huks, like many other guerrilla units at the beginning phases of the war, did not have the means to take on the Japanese army. Evangelista and his men recognized their lack of manpower and support and in turn formulated a battle strategy of small and quick surprise attacks on various Japanese settlements and patrols throughout the regions near Corregidor and Bataan.

Evangelista's political goals included creating a financially independent Philippines free from American governance and capitalism, while most importantly, liberating the Filipi-

---

[91] Robert R. Smith, The Hukbalahap Insurgency: Economic, Political and Military Factors, (Washington, D.C.: Office of the Chief of Military History, 1963), 3-9.

[92] Major Lawrence M. Greenberg, *Historical Analysis Series: THE HUKBALAHAP INSURRECTION, A Case Study of a Successful, Anti-Insurgency Operation in the Philippines, 1946-1955* (Washington D.C.: U.S. Government Printing Office, 1986), 14.

no peasant and working classes.[93] Although Evangelista and members of the PKP (Communist Party of the Philippines, i.e. Partido Komunista ng Filipinas) disagreed with the politics and ideologies of Manuel L. Quezon, the President of the Philippines' Commonwealth (1935-1944), Evangelista and his Huks collaborated with the Allies and other Filipino guerrillas representing the commonwealth throughout the war. Evangelista's guerrillas by the end of the war would consist of a variety of labor oriented recruits. These men and women had political roots and ties to both the socialist and the communist parties, were peasant farmers and workers from the National Peasants' Union and Kapisanang Pambansa ng mga Magbudukid sa Filippinas (KPMP), and were members of the AMT (a worker's union also known as the League of Poor Laborers).[94]

By December 10th, 1941, Evangelista and his guerrillas agreed to officially align themselves with the Allied forces and the Philippines' Commonwealth headed by Quezon. Evangelista's forces were successful not only in their raids across Luzon's northern landscape but also were able to provide the underground resistance with the much needed ammunitions and promote a successful image of Filipino resistance to the Japanese forces winning the support of some Filipino communities of Luzon. Evangelista and his guerrillas' successful raids helped to prompt more Filipino civilians and peasant farmers to join the guerrilla movement throughout the war.

Evangelista was able to recruit en masse, Filipinos who were part of the peasant class in particular. Evangelista's political ideologies that emphasized aiding in liberating the peasantry and farming families, struck a personal chord with the Filipino peoples and Evangelista and his CPP guerrillas were

---

[93] Theodore Friend, *The Blue-Eyed Enemy: Japan Against the West in Java and Luzon, 1942-1945* (New Jersey: Princeton University Press, 2014), 47.

[94] Daniel B. Schirmer and Stephen Rosskamm Shalom, *The Philippines Reader: A History of Colonialism, Neocolonialism, Dictatorship, and Resistance* (Cambridge: South End Press, 1987), 63.

often seen as virtuous bandits helping the poor by attacking the Japanese and the Filipinos who aligned themselves with the Japanese Imperial Army (also known as the Makapili, Filipinos who collaborated with the Japanese in routing out the Filipino underground resistance).[95]

Huk commander, "El Supremo" Luis Taruc, and his Huks looking over a newspaper article on President Truman's actions in the Pacific, 1945, National Library of the Philippines.[96]

With the Japanese execution of Evangelista in 1942, guerilla socialist leader, Luis Taruc, became the Huk Commander. Under his leadership, the Hukbalahaps would continue to compete, absorb, fight, or collaborate with other American and Filipino guerrillas. But for a number of their missions where the Huks would collaborate with Allied forces, such

---

[95] Major Lawrence M. Greenberg, *Historical Analysis Series: THE HUKBALAHAP INSURRECTION, A Case Study of a Successful, Anti-Insurgency Operation in the Philippines, 1946-1955* (Washington D.C.: U.S. Government Printing Office, 1986), 15.

[96] Primo Esteria, "Today in Philippine History, June 21st, 1913, Luis Taruc Was Born in Santa Monica, San Luis, Pampanga," *The Kahimyang Project*, Last Modified June 19th, 2016, Last Accessed July 16th, 2017, https://kahimyang.com/kauswagan/articles/1839/today-in-philippine-history-june-21-1913-luis-taruc-was-born-in-santa-monica-san-luis-pampanga.

as the liberation of the POW and civilian camps throughout Luzon (i.e. the Raid of Cabanatuan and the Raid of Los Banos), Huk units would offer their soldiers as reserves to the U.S. 11th Airborne Division.[97]

Among one of the many organized guerrilla organizations in Luzon, their participation in the underground resistance proved to accelerate the process for the liberation of the Philippines. Despite the setbacks, attacks, and capture of Huks by the Japanese, and the tensions felt amongst USAFFE and other Filipino guerrillas against the Huks, the Huks achieved in organizing and establishing peace in a number of the barrios and villages in Luzon that the Japanese had abandoned as the tide of war in the Pacific turned to favor the Allies.[98]

Hunters ROTC

The Hunter Guerrillas' location of their activities and headquarters could be found throughout Southern Luzon, Manila, and the Laguna de Bay region. The Hunter guerrillas were among one of the main guerrilla organizations that were initially formed by the cadets that once served the Philippine Military Academy prior to the war.[99] Under the order of General MacArthur, the Philippine Military Academy was to be disbanded in 1942, right before the Japanese Imperial Army took control of Manila. The younger soldiers studying and training at the PMA (Philippine Military Academy) wanted desperately to join the war effort despite MacArthur's orders and gathered a substantial amount of recruits who

---

[97] Allyn C. Ryan, *RM: A Biographical Novel of Ramon Magsaysay* (Xlibris Corporation, 2007), 59.

[98] John D. Lukacs, *Escape from Davao: The Forgotten Story of the Most Daring Prison Break of the Pacific War* (New York: NAL Caliber Penguin Group, 2010), 241.

[99] Bruce Henderson, *Rescue at Los Banos: The Most Daring Prison Camp Raid of World War II* (New York: HarperCollins, 2015), 116.

had been part of various ROTC units. Taking what training they had learned from the PMA, the young soldiers schooled their new recruits as saboteurs (ruining phone lines, radio connections, eliminating pro-Japanese Filipinos and spies, and conducting small hit and run raids). One of the youngest guerrilla recruits was the then sixteen year old Mario Montenegro who would become a major film star in Filipino cinema after the war.

A post World War II 1961 Filipino film, starring Hunter ROTC guerrilla veteran Mario Montenegro. The film Karugtong ng Kahapon depicts the struggles and confrontations between Filipino patriots and the Japanese army during the occupation of the Philippines Islands. The film poster reveals the many methods of torture the Japanese military used to extract any information on the underground resistance from both the Filipino civilians and guerrillas.[100]

---

[100] Video 48, "The Sixties, #169," *Video 48: A Virtual Online Library and Archive on Philippine Cinema,* Last Modified Augst 12, 2014, Last Accessed July 9th, 2017, https://www.timetoast.com/timelines/mobilizing-for-wwII.

Filipino 1968 film that depicts the retaking of Manila by Allied forces and Filipino guerrilla units starring a Filipino and Asian American cast starring veteran guerrilla and actor Mario Montenegro.[101]

---

[101] Video 48, "The Sixties: Manila, Open City," *Video 48: A Virtual Online Library and Archive on Philippine Cinema*, Last Modified September 26, 2015, Last Accessed July 8th, 2017, https://video48.blogspot.com/2015/09/the-sixties-1221-charito-solis-james.html?m=1.

A 1983 Philippine stamp that commemorates the founder of the Hunters ROTC guerrillas, Miguel Z. Ver.[102]

The ROTC organization of guerrillas would become one of the few officially recognized Filipino led forces by MacArthur and his staff. Their first phases of recruitment, training, and collection of arms, began in the Antipolo Mountains after the surrender of American and Filipino troops at Corregidor. The founder of the Hunters ROTC was himself a Philippine Military Academy cadet by the name of Miguel Ver who even prior to the surrender of USAFFE at Bataan and Corregidor was already going through the motions of collecting recruits

---

[102] Topical Philippines, "Miguel Ver," *Topical Philippines*, Last Modified 2011, Last Accessed July 20th, 2017, http://topicalphilippines.com/People_Individuals/Ver_Miguel.html.

to fight the impending Japanese invasion.[103] By the end of the war, the Hunters ROTC would collect over 25,000 recruits and serve as the head frontline guerrilla units for the major raid, the Raid of Los Banos in February of 1945 freeing 2,147 Allied POWS.[104]

One of the main leaders of the Hunters ROTC was Colonel Eleuterio Adevoso. At the age of 23, Adevoso served as a prime example of the younger generation of cadets who made up the majority of the Hunter guerrillas. Adevoso would conduct correspondence with one of MacArthur's representatives and head of the General Guerrilla Command, Major Jay D. Vanderpool.[105] But the Hunters guerrillas were not always keen on collaborations amongst all guerrillas seeking to remove the Japanese forces from the Philippines.

The Hunters were known to not always see eye to eye with other guerrilla groups, a common issue pertaining to the tensions felt amongst the politically charged guerrilla groups. The PQOC (President Quezon's Guerrillas) for example were known to butt heads in terms of strategy and political agenda with the Hunters.[106] The Hunters nonetheless, like their other Filipino patriots, could set aside their differences and work towards efficient and collaborative efforts with the American Armed forces, the Philippine Constabulary, the Philippines Commonwealth Army, and various other guerrilla forces (Markings, Huks, Wa Chi, and Bolomen guerrillas) throughout the war.

---

[103] Proculo L. Mojica, *Terry's Hunters: The True Story of the Hunters ROTC Guerrillas* (Benipayo Press, 1965), 29.

[104] Mojica, *Terry's Hunters*, 54, 370, 574.

[105] Supreme Commander of the Allied Powers, General Staff of General MacArthur, *Reports of General MacArthur: The Campaigns of MacArthur in the Pacific, Vol. I.* (Library of Congress, 1966), 80-85. Last Accessed July 9th, 2017, .http://www.history.army.mil/books/wwii/70-42/70-424.html.

[106] Bruce Henderson, *Rescue at Los Banos: The Most Daring Prison Camp Raid of World War II* (New York: HarperCollins, 2015), 182.

A Filipino Newspaper describing the success of the Los Banos Raid of 1945 and the mention of the Filipino and American guerrillas who aided in the attack. The Raid of Los Banos was overshadowed internationally by the American victory of taking Iwo Jima.[107]

According to author Bruce Henderson in his book *Rescue at Los Banos: The Most Daring Prison Camp Raid of World War II*, the Hunters provided the bulk of the fighting force during the 1945 raid to free the POWs and civilians of the camp, Los Banos.[108] The leader in charge of the Hunters guerrillas tasked with heading the raid of Los Banos was Unified Ground Commander, Colonel Honorio K. Guerrero. During the Battle of Manila, the Hunters ROTC guerrilla units under the leadership of Lt. Emmanuel V. de Ocampo from February to March of 1945, would help to secure the capital city and rid the area of any Japanese soldier stragglers with the aid of American guerrillas and USAFFE. One of their finest feats include the only all guerrilla led raid on a Japanese manned

---

[107] Brave Host, "Diary of a POW, Herman Beaber," *POW/MIA Ring*, Last Modified March 27th, 2017, Last Accessed July 7th, 2017, http://ithascome.bravehost.com/.
[108] Henderson, *Rescue at Los Banos*, 181.

prison in Muntinlupa in 1943. Their successful raid allowed for the release of their guerrilla comrades, in particular the honorable Colonel Gustavo Ingles who had been captured and repeatedly tortured and questioned by the Japanese Imperial Army for his reconnaissance work near Manila.[109] By raiding the prison, the Hunter guerrillas were also able to pilfer Japanese arms that helped supply the resistance units of Southeastern Luzon. By the end of the war, the Hunters ROTC were able to secure eleven provinces on Luzon, make numerous contributions to sustaining reconnaissance networks, and were most noted for their cooperativeness among other Filipino patriots and their fellow American peers.[110]

Marking's Guerrillas

Another well established and famed guerrilla organization, the Markings, was led, organized, and founded by Colonel Marcos V. Agustin with the help of his comrade and future wife, Colonel Yay Panlilio. Their organization would be concentrated initially in east of Manila. Compared to the younger ROTC guerrillas, the guerrilla fighters who were recruited under Colonel Augustin, tended to be older civilians and soldiers who were both tenacious fighters and strategists. Similar to the Hunters ROTC, collaboration and cooperative strategies proved to be a reliable trait of the Markings force. Their Allied contributions in taking back the capital would culminate in one of their well known missions: the taking of the Ipo Dam.

The Ipo Dam mission reflected the energy and relentless training that Marking's guerrillas possessed. They worked and trained with the U.S. 43rd Division in taking the Ipo

---

[109] Henderson, *Rescue at Los Banos*, 179-182.
[110] Isagani R. Cruz, *Once a Hunter, Always a Hunter: Jaime N. Ferrer As a Public Servant* (Michigan: Jamie N. Foundation, 1994), 34.

Dam, one of the major dams that supplied the Japanese occupied Manila. Although General Yamashita and his men were already retreating into the northern mountain region of Luzon towards Baguio, Yamashita's retreating strategy was to aggressively defend what resources they had left available to them.[111] The aggressive defense Yamashita and his men would display, forced MacArthur's men and the Filipino guerrillas to fight at various lines ultimately leading to substantial wastes of ammunition and energy, trying to invade and retake the Philippines. This tactic would lead to what Yamashita hoped would prove to drain the resources and desires of the Allied forces and deter them from sacrificing more soldiers to invade mainland Japan and the Ryukyu Islands.[112]

The Markings' remarkable guerrilla operations allowed for multiple advancements for the underground resistance and Philippine morale. One of the most notable achievements of the Markings included the restoration of major water supplies to Manila. Others successes were the stimulation of the Philippine local economies through their printing of Marking banknotes that would fuel both the underground resistance and their local Filipino communities that aligned themselves with the Philippine Commonwealth.[113] The Markings' strong and organized combat missions northeast of Manila allowed for an increase in the spread and production of the Marking Banknotes which helped to fund theirs and the local Filipino communities of Luzon's resistance as Japan tirelessly worked to control both the natural resources and economic output of Philippine goods throughout the war.[114]

---

[111] Mark Berhow & Terrance McGovern, *American Defenses of Corregidor and Manila Bay, 1898-1945* (Bloomsbury Publishing, 2012), 37.

[112] Clayton Chun, *Luzon 1945: The Final Liberation of the Philippines* (Bloomsbury Publishing, 2017), 28-36.

[113] Chun, *Luzon 1945: The Final Liberation of the Philippines*, 39-45.

[114] Supreme Commander of the Allied Powers, General Staff of General MacArthur, *Reports of General MacArthur: The Campaigns of MacArthur in the Pa-*

Collaborations among other guerrilla units during major confrontations with the Japanese Imperial Army produced outstanding results for fending off the Japanese threat and allowing for a smoother entry of MacArthur's forces back into the Philippine islands. The Markings with their combined efforts of working alongside the Hunter ROTC guerrillas, the guerrilla forces captured Japanese spies and those FIlipinos who aligned themselves with the Japanese; the Makapili. In the liberation and Battle of Atimonan, a campaign from January-August 1945, Marking's guerrillas fought alongside the Philippines Commonwealth Army and the PQOG (President Quezon's Organized Guerrillas) contributing nearly 8,400 guerrillas in total to an eight month long ordeal.[115] With the assaults made by both Markings and PQOG guerrillas, the major city of Atimonan, Tayabas was retaken, allowing for the official takeover of American forces and the declaration that the area was now controlled by both the U.S. military and Philippine Commonwealth in August of 1945.

---

cific, Vol. I. (Library of Congress, 1966), 319-320.

[115] Shelby L. Stanton, *Order of Battle: U.S. Army, World War II* (Presidio Press, 1984), 95.

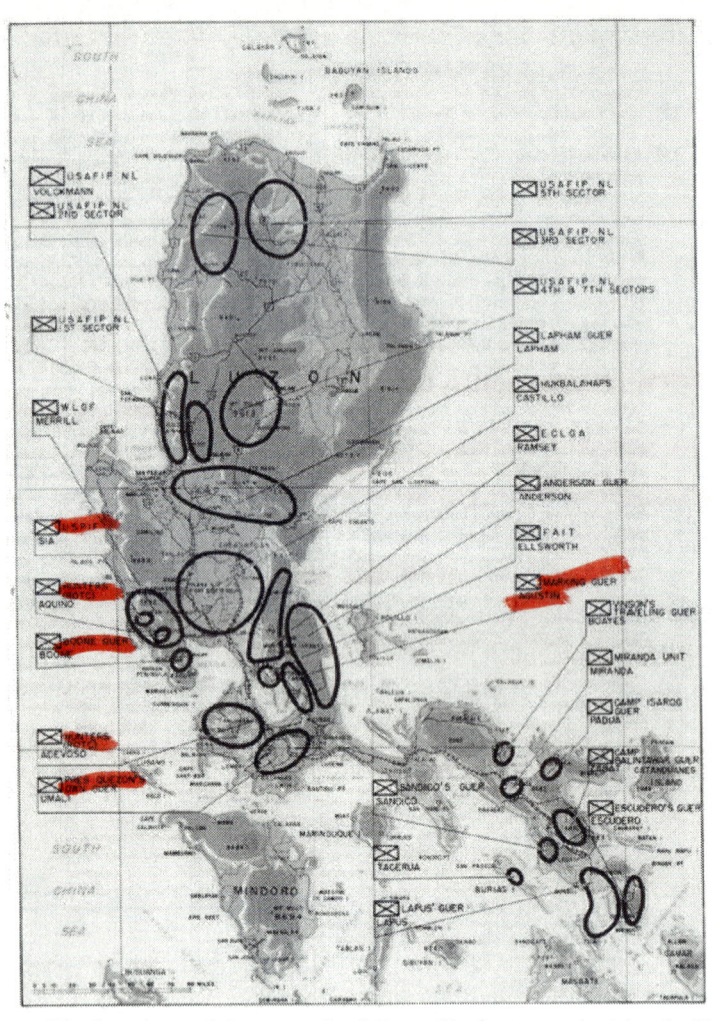

The locations of the recognized Guerrilla forces on the island of Luzon, 1944.[116]

---

[116] Supreme Commander of the Allied Powers, General Staff of General MacArthur, *Reports of General MacArthur: The Campaigns of MacArthur in the Pacific, Vol. I.* (Library of Congress, 1966), 319.

United States Army Forces in the Philippines of Northern Luzon (USAFIP-NL)

The United States Army Forces of Northern Luzon (USAFIP-NL) was compiled of both American and Filipino soldiers and guerrillas. The organized task force was led and commanded by General Russel W. Volckmann. USAFIP-NL served as a military force that numbered more than 8000 infantrymen, hailing from the 11th, 14th, 15th, 66th, and the 121st Infantry Regiments.[117] The Filipino guerrillas under Volckmann's leadership were made up of various Filipino ethnic minorities from the northern cordilleras/mountain passes and ranges. The northern guerrillas' knowledge of the mountainous terrain was crucial in helping to eliminate the last stronghold of the Japanese military out of Northern Luzon, the regions near and surrounding Baguio City, and the Japanese surrender in September of 1945. In total, the guerrillas that served with Volckmann's USAFIP-NL were successful in regaining the Northern Philippine regions from the Japanese in the battles of Bacsil Ridge (March, 1945), Baguio (April, 1945), of Bessang Pass (June, 1945), and of Kiangan (September, 1945) all within in one year.

The back to back military successes owe a great deal to the efforts of the Filipino ethnic and indigenous guerrillas, especially in the Battle of Kiangan. In this final and decisive battle that forced the eventual surrender of General Yamashita, guerrilla units had restored Allied networks of communication in the province of Ilocos Sur. Furthermore, the USAFIP-NL guerrillas cut off all the escape routes left for the remaining Imperial Japanese Army led by General Tomoyuki Yamashita. The USAFIP-NL's main task of notifying and

---

[117] Robert Ross Smith & the Defense Dept., Army, Center of Military History, *US Army in World War II, War in the Pacific, Triumph in the Philippines* (Washington D.C.: Center of Military History - United States Army, 1993), 556.

directing civilians in the surrounding towns of Ilocos Sur to evacuate and find shelter prior to the American bombing of the area is one such understated act of heroism that saved thousands of lives from friendly fire and the heavy artillery fired by desperate Japanese soldiers.[118]

Ethnic Minorities: Negritos, Igorot Mountain Hunters, Chinese Nationalists, & the Muslim fighters of Mindanao

> For a personal recollection of the Filipino military perspective, watch Filipino Soldier, Lieutenant Francisco Balanban retell the guerrilla and ethnic Ifugao minority efforts and experience in the decisive battle of Kiangan. Source: Newslife, "Battle of Kiangan," *People's Television Network Inc. Philippines*, https://www.youtube.com/watch?v=3crjCzWBg4A.

The guerrillas of Northern Luzon in particular did not always have the benefit of geographically being near MacArthur and his reconnaissance team in the South Pacific. The distance between the the guerrillas of Northern Luzon and General MacArthur in the South Pacific meant that military and supplemental resources were not always available or secured. The mountainous and forested terrain of Northern Luzon on the other hand did prove to be a strategic advantage despite the lack of secure networks of communication with MacArthur.

In Northern Luzon, the cordilleras encompass various Philippine ethnic minorities whom have their own dialects, religious and cultural traditions. The mountain province peoples known for their unique dialects and intricate woodcarving and textile work make up a significant bulk of the ethnic minorities who served as guerrillas in the uppermost region of Northern Luzon. Many acted as guides for Bataan escapees and resistance fighters. Other served as combatants,

---

[118] Real Sons and Daughters of Ifugao, "Battle of Kiangan: The Pacific Battle of World War II Ended Here," *RSDI Freedom Wall*, Last Modified February 8th, 2016, Last Accessed July 8th, 2017, http://www.armchairgeneral.com/trek-to-kiangan-and-back.htm.

spies, and saboteurs for the Allies and took part in the major battles, such as the Battle of Kiangan, that focused on the retaking of Northern and Central Luzon.

The Negrito Special Troops (All Aeta Squadron 30) photographed in Tarlac Province, 1945.[119]

The Aetas

One of the major, however lesser known, indigenous guerrilla units that served in Northern and Central Luzon were the Aetas. The Aetas are a Negrito ethnic group considered to be one of the earliest inhabitants of the Philippine Islands. The Aeta Negritos were geographically isolated from the urban cities and main provinces of Luzon, which meant that their knowledge of the mountain regions of Luzon, their understanding of the local natural resources, and their hunting and tracking skills, were considerably valuable resources to the underground resistance.[120] Aeta guerrillas like

---

[119] Tonnette Orejas, "Pension Elusive for Aeta Guerrillas," *Philippine Daily Inquirer, Inquirer.net*, Last Modified March 2, 2016, Last Accessed July 9th, 2017, http://newsinfo.inquirer.net/769917/pension-elusive-for-aeta-guerrillas.

[120] Peter Eisner, *MacArthur's Spies: The Soldier, the Singer, and the Spymaster who Defied the Japanese in World War II* (New York: Viking-Penguin Random House, 2017), 41, 42, 46, 242.

Emiliano Sanchez and his brother in law Romano Sanchez were just one example of the pockets of indigenous guerrillas who served in the all Aeta Squadron in Tarlac Province, led initially by Captain Alfred Bruce, throughout the Japanese occupation.[121]

The Aeta Squadron 30 consisted of over 100 Aeta guerrillas. Their tasks included hiding and protecting American guerrilla leaders and American soldiers in the mountain caves of Bagingan of upper Mataba.[122] When food supplies ran out, in order to feed the American and Filipino soldiers and guerrillas, the Aeta squadron grew tubers (sweet potatoes and yams) and rice to feed their units often raiding Japanese controlled food supplies as well. The Aeta guerrillas also helped American pilots whose planes had been shot down by Japanese bombers in Luzon, guarded the guerrilla road networks, and routed out Japanese soldiers hiding in the mountains in man made dugouts.[123]

Other indigenous groups that would contribute to the guerrilla resistance were the Igorots, an Austronesian ethnic group of the highland mountain provinces of Northern Luzon. Similar to the Aetas, the Igorots dwelled far from the more urban regions of Luzon and were also valuable to the resistance in terms of their knowledge of the difficult mountain terrain and its various natural resources. Trained and led by Lt. Col. Russel W. Volckmann, a leader of the Philippine Commonwealth Army and guerrilla resistance of Northern Luzon, Igorot tribesmen guerrilla duties included demolition (strategic bombing of major structures), and would act

---

[121] Tonnette Orejas, "Pension Elusive for Aeta Guerrillas," *Philippine Daily Inquirer, Inquirer.net*, Last Modified March 2, 2016, Last Accessed July 9th, 2017, http://newsinfo.inquirer.net/769917/pension-elusive-for-aeta-guerrillas.

[122] Tonnette Orejas, "Pension Elusive for Aeta Guerrillas."

[123] Tonnette Orejas, "Pension Elusive for Aeta Guerrillas."

as guides and transporters for the American soldiers and guerrillas not familiar with the terrain.[124]

A major Igorot unit that has received little press is Blackburn's Headhunters led by Army Captain Donald D. Blackburn (he would become a Brigadier General after the war). Their efforts would lead to the retaking of the western provinces of Luzon, the Cagayan Valley, and a major sea-port, Aparri. A relatively small unit of guerrillas, the headhunter guerrillas were a skilled, resourceful, and stealthy force that were able to fight and fend off the Japanese 14th Army regiment, despite being outnumbered by them, as demonstrated in the campaign for the retaking of the Cagayan River.[125]

Igorot tribe and village leaders like the noted Kamayong, chief of the Haliap tribe located in Ifugao, would become major contributors to the guerrilla movement in the cordilleras. Kamayong and other Igorot leaders would offer their homes and villages as safe zones for Volckmann's guerrilla camps and would also help strategize effective plans to route out the Japanese armies that brutalized their mountain provinces.[126] Armed with bolos and little else, the Igorots were relentless fighters skilled in both their traditional fighting and hunting styles and were keen marksman with what firepower they were armed with by Volckmann and Blackburn.[127] Overall, the contributions of the minority indigenous groups of Northern Luzon to the resistance would not only allow American guerrilla leaders an advantage of cutting off Japanese forces in the harsh cordillera terrain, but would conclusively allow for more resistance recruits and a much needed

---

[124] Mike Guardia, *American Guerrilla: The Forgotten Heroics of Robert W. Volckmann-The Man Who Escaped from Bataan, Raised a Filipino Army Against the Japanese, and Became the True "Father" of the Army Special Forces*. (Havertown: Casemate Publishing, 2010), location Chapter 9.

[125] Mike Guardia, *Shadow Commander: The Epic Story of Donald D. Blackburn, Guerrilla Leader and Special Forces Leader* (Havertown: Casemate Publishers, 2011), 91-108.

[126] Guardia, *Shadow Commander*, 86, 87.

[127] Guardia, *Shadow Commander*, 63, 87, 99, 108.

unification and collaboration amongst the more marginalized communities of the Philippines, towards a goal of liberation from the invading Japanese.

The 10th Military District and Its Ethnic and Religious Components

U.S. Army corps mining engineer, Wendell Fertig, served as the leader of the guerrilla units located on Mindanao, the southern main island of the Philippines. Fertig's 10th military district served as an organization of guerrillas that within three years would represent up to six military divisions throughout Mindanao and number to over 35,000 men and women that would experience insurmountable odds in their goal of reducing the Japanese force in the South.[128] Fertig's attempts at establishing a unified guerrilla force included daily encounters with hostile Japanese forces intent on eliminating a guerrilla network. Centuries of ethnic and religious feuds amongst the people of Mindanao, guerrilla rivalries, and an unforgiving treacherous jungle landscape were the reality of what Fertig's officers had to operate and navigate in.

One of Fertig's challenges in maintaining both a successful and cohesive fighting force was keeping the peace between the Filipino Muslim and Filipino Christian guerrillas. The Moro are Filipino Muslims who had inhabited the islands of Mindanao, Sulu, and Palawan prior the arrival of the Spanish who had named the Muslim communities of the southern islands as Moors, or Moro, the traditional term medieval Spain associated with Iberian and North African Muslims.[129] The Moro prior to the Spanish American War always served as a

---

[128] Kent Holmes, *Wendell Fertig and His Guerrilla Forces in the Philippines: Fighting the Japanese Occupation, 1942-1945* (Jefferson: McFarland & Company, 2015), 104.

[129] Benjamin R. Beede, *The War of 1898, and U.S. Interventions, 1898-1934, an Encyclopedia* (New York: Garland Publishing Inc., 1994), 347.

rebelling force against Western colonizers and imperialists. When the United States gained the Philippines as a territory from Spain in the aftermath of the Spanish American War, American military leaders of the early twentieth century sought to alleviate the ethnic and religious tensions felt in the southern Philippine Islands. This attempt at improving religious and cultural animosities and rivalries forced the American military to use both "force and fairness" allowing the Moros to practice their religion while maintaining little to no governance over parts of their ancestral homes.[130]

Once the Japanese had taken Luzon's Bataan and Corregidor, the Moros and Christian Filipinos fell into a small civil war. The Moros viewed the surrender of American-Filipino forces as an opportunity to take back lands their ancestors and predecessors had sold to the Christian Filipinos as well as establish their dominance without the hindrance of Western charters or interference.[131]

Realizing that cooperation was key in creating a strong and unified force of Filipino guerrillas in Mindanao, Fertig and other Filipino guerrillas who represented the religious, ethnic, and cultural diversity of Mindanao, not only worked towards liberating the Philippine Islands, but also their efforts helped to pioneer the possibility of a unified and sovereign Philippine state. Among the diverse Filipino guerrilla organizers and leaders of Mindanao, was Datu Umpa. Datu Umpa was a Moro chief, who negotiated a peace treaty with Fertig and was one of the first Moro leaders to consider ending Moro ethnic group rivalries with the American soldiers and Filipino Christians in Mindanao.[132] Datu Umpa's Moros would serve in the 108th Division where the enlisted guerrillas made up a significant armed force of Moros of the Maranao Militia Force under Lt. Colonel Charles W. Hedges.

---

[130] Holmes, *Wendell Fertig and His Guerrilla Forces in the Philippines*, 4.
[131] Holmes, *Wendell Fertig and His Guerrilla Forces in the Philippines*, 4.
[132] Holmes, *Wendell Fertig and His Guerrilla Forces*, 33.

William Tait, a guerrilla fighter of African American and Moro ancestry, also served with Fertig. Tait would help recruit Filipinos, both Christian and Moro to aid the underground resistance and directly arranged with Fertig Mindanao various guerrilla operations and strategies. Tait posed early in the war as an informant to the Japanese Imperial Army. Gaining the trust of the Japanese, Tait stole the much needed weapons, supplies, and valuable information regarding Japanese military strategies and their garrisons leaking it to the Filipino opposition.[133] Guerrilla Lt. Col. Luis Morgan, a mestizo of Filipino and Anglo American ancestry, served as Fertig's chief of staff and helped to establish the initial units of Fertig's guerrilla forces despite his disagreements in leadership tactics with Fertig.[134]

Another lesser known Filipino Muslim guerrilla leader is Datu Busran Kulaw. Kulaw was a Maranao, an ethnic Filipino Muslim group that lives on the southern islands of the Philippines, particularly Mindanao. His unit, Fighting Bolo Battalion Unit, fought the Japanese wherever they encountered one another in the province of Lanao del Sur.[135] Similar to his Moro peers, Kulaw's guerrillas wielded terrifying blades using both guerrilla and juramentado warfare strategies.[136] Juramentado often refers to a male Moro swordsman whose method of fighting involved using bladed weapons, and whose purpose was to fight and die if necessary to fulfill their religious purpose of warding off either belligerent non-believers or those who invaded their ancestral lands.[137] These strategies were so terrifying and successful against the Japanese, that many Japanese found the Moro fighters fierce

---

[133] Holmes, *Wendell Fertig and His Guerrilla Forces*, 28.
[134] John Keats, *They Fought Alone* (Pickles Partners Publishing, 2015).
[135] John Keats, *They Fought Alone: Classics of World War II* (Pennsylvania State University: Time-Life, 2005), 354.
[136] Alan R. Luga, *Muslim Insurgency in Mindanao, Philippines: A Thesis*, Philippine Military Academy, Baguio City, 1981, 3, 16.
[137] Luga, *Muslim Insurgency in Mindanao*, 16.

and nightmarish. Kulaw's Maranao group among other Moro guerrilla units were so successful in their truculent methods of fighting that many Moro communities had retaken and pushed out the Japanese threat out from their ancestral lands prior to the arrival of MacArthur's famous arrival at Red Beach on the island of Leyte on October 1944.[138]

Kulaw's greatest achievement as a Maranao guerilla leader was in establishing a peaceful community, the city known as Wao. Wao after the war would represent an amicable hub that housed both Filipino Christians and Moros.[139] The ethnic, cultural, and religious diversity found among both Fertig's leading officers and Mindanao's other respective Moro guerrillas points to the overwhelming morale of the Filipino resistance despite nearly centuries of ethnic and religious based skirmishes and contentions.

Fertig's Filipino guerrillas like other resistance units in Luzon were forced to make do with what resources were available to them while also maintaining the well being and safety of not only their forces but the surrounding civilian communities. Mindanao Filipino guerrillas helped to establish local governments to oversee and manage villager's needs and the distribution of food and supplies to civilians.[140] With a faltering economy, Fertig's guerrillas printed money with the approval of the exiled president of the Philippine Commonwealth, Manuel Quezon.[141] The guerrillas under Fertig also created small businesses that would repair rifles, cartridges, and would create new cartridges from salvaged metal curtain rods.[142] The Japanese manipulated agrarian exports and shut

---

[138] Andrew H. Tan, *A Handbook of Terrorism and Insurgency in Southeast Asia* (Northampton: Edward Elgar Publishing, 2009), 197.

[139] Hilario Molijan Gomez, *The Moro Rebellion and the Search for Peace: A Study on Christian-Muslim Relations in the Philippines* (Silsilah Publications, 2000), 94, 133.

[140] Holmes, *Wendell Fertig and His Guerrilla Forces*, 58.

[141] Jose D. Aviado, *The Foundation of Philippine Democracy* (University of California Press-Lexicon, 1960), 147.

[142] Major Peter T. Sinclair II, *Men of Destiny: The American and Filipino Guerril-

down all major businesses in an attempt to force the Philippines into both a starved and stagnant economic position.[143] Fertig's guerrillas were responsible for organizing household industries (textiles, alcohol, salt, and oil refining) and small farm units that would provide food supplies for both civilians and guerrillas in Mindanao.

Fertig's guerrillas were as resourceful and organized in taking on civic duties as they were in securing little to no casualties, making use of what artillery and manpower was available even in the most dire circumstances. In various battles and confrontations with the Japanese, Fertig's Filipino guerrillas from 1943-1945 inflicted more casualties on the Japanese than the Japanese had inflicted to the guerrillas. In the Mina-Ano Encounter of January 1945, Lt. Col. Grinstead's 110th Division prevented Japanese reinforcements from joining their garrison in the Butuan region. 160 Japanese soldiers were killed or wounded in this encounter while only one guerrilla was wounded.[144] The Talisayan Operation of March 1945 was an offensive military collaboration between the U.S. Navy and guerrillas of the 110th Infantry Regiment of the 110th Division under Lt. Col. Marshall. The amphibious operation sought to destroy the Japanese garrison in Talisayan (a municipality of the Misamis Oriental Province of Mindanao) that served as a valuable barge staging area for the enemy. The successful operation led to 138 Japanese casualties and zero U.S. Navy and guerrilla losses.[145]

Mindanao would prove to be one of the more difficult Philippine Islands to retake from the Japanese, similar to the cordilleras of Northern Luzon, because of the harsh environmental terrain. The campaign for the Allies' attempt to re-

---

las During the Japanese Occupation of the Philippines: A Monograph by Major Peter T. Sinclair II (Fort Leavenworth: School of Advanced Military Studies, United States Army Command and General Staff College, 2011), 45.

[143] Holmes, *Wendell Fertig and His Guerrilla Forces*, 45-47.
[144] Holmes, *Wendell Fertig and His Guerrilla Forces*, 111-120.
[145] Holmes, *Wendell Fertig and His Guerrilla Forces*, 119.

take Mindanao would span from March of 1945 to August of 1945. The bloody battles that would ensue in and along the borders of the major city of Davao required the collaborative efforts of Fertig's guerrillas, the Philippine Commonwealth Army, the Philippine Constabulary, and the United States' 24th Infantry Division. The final campaign for the complete liberation of the Philippines culminated in the total retaking of Mindanao. The total amount of casualties of the American forces on Mindanao is estimated at nearly 900 men and nearly 3,000 men wounded in battle.[146] These American casualties in comparison to the Japanese casualties of nearly 13,000 (roughly 8,300 dying from wounds, starvation, and disease) reveal just how effective and noteworthy the guerrillas' contributions and strategizing was, resulting in low American casualties.[147] Therefore, the military operations led by Fertig's ethnically, culturally, and religiously diverse guerrillas would ultimately become the necessary manpower that made the Allies' retaking of Mindanao swift and efficient.

The guerrilla units located on Mindanao were deemed so resourceful and efficient in combat in dense jungle terrain that their histories, experiences, and military strategies would serve as the backbone for the military strategizing in the Vietnam War. America's Secret War in Laos (an extension of America's involvement in curbing communist sympathies in Vietnam and Laos' Civil War) would similarly rely on the recruitment of ethnic minorities like the Hmong located throughout East and Southeast Asia. These ethnic minorities and their experiences, similar to the guerrilla makeup of Mindanao, would serve as soldiers during the America's Vietnam Campaign and for many years during America's Cold War efforts in Southeast Asia.[148]

---

[146] Robert Ross Smith, *Triumph in the Philippines: The War in the Pacific, United States Army in World War II.: War In the Pacific* (University Press of the Pacific, 2005), 648, 692.

[147] Smith, *Triumph in the Philippines*, 648-655.

[148] Holmes, *Wendell Fertig and His Guerrilla Forces*, 186, 187.

The Legacy of Fertig

Wendell Fertig in the history of the Mindanao's underground resistance (1942-1945) during World War II would serve as the face of the southern guerrilla movement. Many of the Filipino ethnic guerrilla leaders and fighters continue to remain either nameless faces in surviving photographs of the campaign in Mindanao or receive very little reference. Other secondary sources or popular histories like John Keats *They Fought Alone: A True Story of a Modern Hero* (1963) or Robert Smith's *Triumph in the Philippines* (1963) simply skip over individual Filipino guerrilla contributions and leaders and categorize all Filipino military forces outside of the official USAFFE units as "Filipino Guerrillas" associated with Mindanao. Furthermore, the post war era would experience clashes amongst different separatist political and cultural organizations that would fight to create their own sovereign southern Philippine region.[149] The combined lack of recognition not afforded to the diverse Mindanao guerrillas as well as the cultural, political, and religious based separatist movements of the post war era would place setbacks in recognizing and researching the historical impact of the Filipino guerrillas in the liberation of the Pacific.

---

[149] Sinclair II, *Men of Destiny*, 62.

Chinese and Filipino-Chinese Nationalist Guerrilla Units

A photo of Filipino, Filipino-Chinese, and Chinese guerrillas guarding Japanese captured soldiers on Luzon.[150]

Chinese ethnic guerrillas could be found throughout the lowland provinces near Manila on the island of Luzon throughout the war. These guerrilla units were known as the Ampaw Unit led by Colonel Chua Sy Tiao and the 48th Squadron also known as the Wa Chi (other resources spell their unit as Wha Chi) founded May 19th, 1942.[151] Colonel Chua Sy Tiao led the Ampaw, which were initially an intelligence guerrilla subunit of Marking's guerrillas. Their

---

[150] "The Wa Chi Movement," *Watawat*, Last Accessed July 20th, 2017, http://www.watawat.net/the_wa_chi_movement.html.

[151] Ida Anita Q. del Mundo, "Wha Chi 48th Squadron's 70th Anniversary: Herois & Friendship," *Philstar Global*, Last Modified June 3rd, 2012, Last Accessed August 4th, 2017, http://www.philstar.com/starweek-magazine/813000/wha-chi-48th-squadrons-70th-anniversary-heroism-and-friendship.

name, Ampaw, translates to the street food dish "puff rice" and became the nickname of the unit because of their undercover spy network in Manila disguised as puff rice street vendors.[152] The Ampaw was founded in Antipolo, Rizal (the Sierra Madre Mountain region) and made up particularly of mestizo Filipinos who had Chinese ancestry and were were nicknamed Chilipinos.[153]

Although a rather small unit of less than 1000 men, the Chilipinos of the Ampaw provided the much needed intelligence networks to survey both Manila under Japanese occupation and the rough terrain of the Sierra Madre mountains. The Ampaw also scavenged the region for food and arms for the Marking guerrillas and aided POW and straggler USAFFE soldiers who would later join the resistance movement. The Ampaw were also assigned in protecting and maintaining spy networks in over ten major towns of southeastern Luzon (Manila City, Tanay, Pasay, Pasig, Montalban, Morong, San Guillermo, Taytay, Teresa, and Pililia).[154]

Chinese immigrants faced more severe cases of discrimination and interrogation from Japanese soldiers who believed that Chinese immigrants were more prone to joining guerrilla and resistance movements in the Philippines due to the Japanese occupation of mainland China.[155] Colonel Chua, like many of the Chinese guerrillas he organized, was part of the Chinese Nationalist Army and party (Kuomint-

---

[152] Colonel Frank B. Quesada, "Balitang Beterano: Filipino-Chinese Guerrilla In WWII," *Philippine Headline News Online*, http://www.newsflash.org/2004/02/tl/tl012495.htm.

[153] Quesada, "Balitang Beterano: Filipino-Chinese Guerrilla In WWII," *Philippine Headline News Online*, http://www.newsflash.org/2004/02/tl/tl012495.htm.

[154] Colonel Frank B. Quesada, "Balitang Beterano: Filipino-Chinese Guerrilla In WWII," *Philippine Headline News Online*, http://www.newsflash.org/2004/02/tl/tl012495.htm.

[155] Colonel Frank B. Quesada, "Balitang Beterano: Filipino-Chinese Guerrilla In WWII," *Philippine Headline News Online*, http://www.newsflash.org/2004/02/tl/tl012495.htm.

ang) and fought for the liberation of the Philippines so as to prevent the atrocities in China from occurring elsewhere. Chinese soldiers were forewarned about the impending Japanese pan-Asian invasion of the Pacific and were sent, or volunteered, to prevent the atrocities, like the 1937-1938 Rape of Nanking, from occurring elsewhere in the Pacific.

Other Chinese immigrants who would make up the various Chinese Filipino guerrilla units were young men who sought to better their lives and those of their families by working abroad in the Philippines like the Chinese guerrilla, Dee Hong Ki, of the Wa Chi unit.[156] At the age of 13, Dee Hong Ki immigrated to the Philippines in 1936 for better economic opportunities leaving civil war ridden China to make a mark in a small business in the Philippines. A year after Dee Hong Ki's migration to the Philippine Islands, his hometown Peiping would be invaded. China's occupation by the Japanese Imperial Army proved to be a warning to Western interests in the Pacific to be on guard for their long held Asian territories (Burma, Vietnam/Indochine, Malays, Philippines, etc). Chinese immigrants, like Dee Hong Ki, in response to the increasing presence of Imperialist Japan, would send money to their homelands to help fuel the anti-Japanese resistance on Chinese soil prior to the Filipino American surrender of Corregidor.[157] Chinese immigrants like Dee Hong Ki who had established the Philippines as their home joined the guerrilla underground resistance movement both to avenge their native country, as well as to protect and liberate their new homeland. Dee Hong Ki and his brother joined the Wa Chi, and as guerrillas, took on a number of missions involving staving off Japanese patrol units in the agrarian

---

[156] ABS-CBN News, "How Chinese Fought for Philippine Freedom," *ABS-CBN News*, Last Modified November 3rd, 2016, Last Accessed July 20th, 2017, http://news.abs-cbn.com/focus/02/19/15/how-chinese-guerrillas-fought-philippine-freedom.

[157] ABS-CBN News, "How Chinese Fought for Philippine Freedom."

fields southeast of Manila (Santa Cruz & San Pablo) and defending villagers and farmers from the Japanese forces.[158]

The Chinese guerrilla unit, Wa Chi, consisted of 1000 soldiers who were Filipinos with Chinese ancestry, Chinese Nationalist soldiers, or were Chinese immigrants who shared the common goal of liberating the Philippine peoples from the Japanese Imperial Army.[159] Other members of the Chinese guerrilla units were previous members of the United Workers Union of Manila who sought to rally civilians outside of the city against the Japanese Imperial presence.[160] Still other labor oriented organizations that collaborated with the Wa Chi were the socialist and communist Huks who, in part, helped to both fund and establish the Wa Chi Chinese unit that would operate on Bulacan and Laguna.[161]

Chinese guerrillas had to be extra careful and strategically placed in order to avoid being mistaken as Japanese soldiers and shot at by friendly fire. During the meetings between the guerrilla and USAFFE leaders in regards to the raids, it was decided that the Chinese guerrilla units would have to be kept out of fights with the Japanese in order to avoid any confusion for being mistaken as Japanese themselves in the chaos of the battlefields.[162] The Filipino-Chinese 48th Squad-

---

[158] ABS-CBN News, "How Chinese Fought for Philippine Freedom," *ABS-CBN News*, Last Modified November 3rd, 2016, Last Accessed July 20th, 2017, http://news.abs-cbn.com/focus/02/19/15/how-chinese-guerrillas-fought-philippine-freedom.

[159] ABS-CBN News, "How Chinese Fought for Philippine Freedom," *ABS-CBN News*, Last Modified November 3rd, 2016, Last Accessed July 20th, 2017, http://news.abs-cbn.com/focus/02/19/15/how-chinese-guerrillas-fought-philippine-freedom.

[160] Fannie Tan Koa, "The Wha-Chi Guerrillas," *The Philippine Star Global*, Last Modified May 24th, 2015, Last Accessed July 30th, 2017, http://www.philstar.com/starweek-magazine/2015/05/24/1457950/wha-chi-guerilas.

[161] Major Lawrence M. Greenberg, *Historical Analysis Series: THE HUKBALAHAP INSURRECTION, A Case Study of a Successful, Anti-Insurgency Operation in the Philippines, 1946-1955* (Washington D.C.: U.S. Government Printing Office, 1986), 20.

[162] Bruce Henderson, *Rescue at Los Banos: The Most Daring Prison Camp Raid of World War II*. (New York: HarperCollins, 2015), 164, 182, 215, 216.

ron thus served as guards along the paths and highways that the various guerrilla units would use throughout the duration of the raids from 1944-1945.[163] By collaborating with the Hunters ROTC, Marking's Guerrillas, and the Huks, as early as 1943, the success of the smaller Chinese-Filipino guerrilla units are a significant representation of the ethnic and political inclusivity, and diversity, that made up the Philippine underground resistance.

As an ethnic minority within the Philippines, the Chinese and Chinese-Filipino guerrillas would receive even less attention than their Filipino guerrilla peers in receiving credit or acknowledgment as to their contribution to the underground resistance. Despite despite their lack of recognition in the historical narrative of the liberation of the Philippines, historic landmarks and markers throughout Central Luzon serve as evidence of the heroism of the Chinese guerrillas. Small monuments, community organizations, memorials, and school buildings located throughout Manila's historical Chinatown are small dedications and reminders of the Wa Chi guerrillas who protected the townspeople, cities, and provinces of Central Luzon.

---

[163] Henderson, *Rescue at Los Banos*, 215, 216.

A World War II memorial marker that honors the heroics of the Filipino and Chinese guerrillas of the 48th Squadron during the Second Battle of Santa Cruz on January 26th, 1945. The marker is located in Santa Cruz, a municipality of the province of Laguna in Luzon.[164]

Conclusion

Only a certain number of groups were recognized by General MacArthur as guerrilla fighters serving in the Pacific.

---

[164] Ramon F Velasquez, (Own work) [CC BY-SA 3.0 (http://creativecommons.org/licenses/by-sa/3.0)], via Wikimedia Commons, *Wikimedia Commons*, Last Modified August 13th, 2015, Last Accessed July 30th, 2017, https://commons.wikimedia.org/wiki/File%3ABattleofSantaCruzjf9467_02.JPG.

Only those associated within specific military districts and units would be allowed to receive veteran benefits and recognition after the war. Proving one's military status during the war continues to be an arduous and timely task. Many who served in remote areas of the Philippines where military records were poorly maintained, if at all, have a difficult time procuring the necessary documentation to prove their veteran status. Also, many guerrilla fighters that had died in battle, or were captured and executed by the Japanese, were left no time or opportunity to record their roles and which respective units they represented. These predicaments in terms of keeping official guerrilla records has led to roadblocks for guerrillas and their families to gain any honorable mention or recognition as war veterans. This issue has caused many families to argue legally for pensions that their veteran family members deserve. Also, the monetary means of proving one's role legally has proven to be rather expensive especially for ethnic minorities like the Aeta who traditionally earn a subsistence living by managing their ancestral lands in an ever commercially growing developing country like the Philippines.

Although American military records are typically thorough and extensive, not all guerrillas during the Japanese occupation were recorded. Often times, records of guerrilla fighters were not kept or stored because members of the underground resistance were aware of the secrecy that had to be maintained about their plans in case the Japanese secret police would discover their networks of comrades and communication.[165] Memoirs and oral histories can help prove and provide the roles and names of the numerous guerrilla leaders and soldiers that aided the American and Australian Allies. However, the ethnic guerrillas mentioned in many

---

[165] Major Peter T. Sinclair, II, *Men of Destiny: The American and Filipino Guerrillas During the Japanese Occupation of the Philippines*, A Monograph (Fort Leavenworth: School of Advanced Military Studies, 2011), 7.

American memoirs and histories give little to no mention of Filipino guerrillas' names. What is often highlighted or recalled are the Filipino guerrillas' overall tenacity, craftiness to make do with what little supplies they had, and their courage.

Despite these honorable mentions in character, popular narratives in regards to the retaking of the Philippines and the defeat of the Japanese Imperial Navy and Army do not directly mention the total and expansive efforts of all the Filipino guerrilla units. The lack of names and references to all the guerrilla units reflects the victory as mainly an American organized and led victory, not necessarily a victory that required the collaboration and grassroots resistance that the Filipino guerrillas had collected and mobilized throughout the war. By addressing attention to the lack of recognition to Filipino resistance fighters during the war, the task of re-assessing and rewriting popular World War II historical narratives to include people of color and other minorities becomes imperative as it confirms the complexity and diversity of global conflicts. Furthermore, traditional World War II histories that seek to include the mention of the Filipino underground resistance would finally answer the noble cause in paying overdue gratitude and respect to all the sacrifices of the survivors and veterans of the Pacific Theater.

Other Resources

For more information on similar topics that this chapter addresses, please check these alternative resources:

Public Military Archives:
A total list of the guerrilla units recognized by the American Military's National Archives: https://www.archives.gov/research/military/ww2/philippine/guerrilla-list-2.html.

Film & Documentaries:
Unsurrendered 2, written and directed by Bani Lograno, is a documentary film that showcases the efforts of the Hunters ROTC guerrillas and their fellow American and Chinese insurgents of World War II. For more videos, photos, and information of the production visit: https://www.facebook.com/Spyron.AVManila/.

The Great Raid directed by John Dahl is a 2005 historical film that depicts the efforts of the Allied Forces and Philippine guerrilla fighters in the planning and execution of the famous raid, the Raid of Cabantuan.[166]

---

[166] *The Great Raid*, directed by John Daul, featuring Benjamin Bratt and James Franco, produced by Miramax, 2005.

The Atrocities

The Filipino and American POWs begin the Death March. Thousands would die along the way. [167]

---

[167] National Museum of the Air Force. "Bataan Death March." Official United States Air Force Website. Last modified April 29, 2015. Last accessed July 31, 2017. http://www.nationalmuseum.af.mil/Visit/Museum-Exhibits/Fact-Sheets/Display/Article/196797/bataan-death-march/

CHAPTER 4
Bataan Death March

The Death March of Bataan following the Battle of Bataan on April 9th, 1942 remains one of the infamous atrocities committed in Asia during World War II. The Japanese had not anticipated the large number of captured prisoners, approximately 78,000 captives (12,000 American, 60,000-70,000 Filipino)[168], and transporting the American and Filipino soldiers to prisoner of war (POW) camps became a logistical nightmare. Following General King's surrender, Japanese General Nakayama assured King that the American and Filipino captives would be treated well. The following succession of events would become a gross contradiction of Nakayama's word.

---

[168] Chun, *The Fall of the Philippines 1941-1942*, 77.

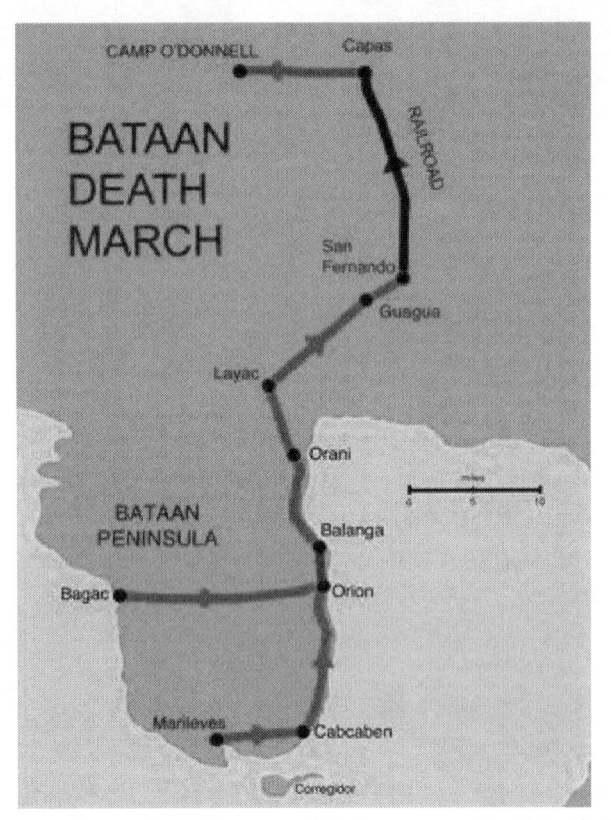

The route from where the men of Bataan surrendered to their final destination was a total of about 65-70 miles. Once arriving to the San Fernando trailhead, the men would take a train to Capas, where they marched a final nine miles to Camp O'Donnell. [169]

In preparation to march north away from Corregidor, the Japanese first looted the American and Filipino prisoners of their possessions. If found with Japanese mementos or money, prisoners would be punished, sometimes killed.[170] One of the first atrocities of the march was the Pantingan massacre of approximately 400 Filipino officers of the Philippine Army

---

[169] "Bataan Death March," National Museum of the US Air Force.
[170] Michael Norman and Elizabeth M. Norman, *Tears in the Darkness: The Story of the Bataan Death March and its aftermath* (New York: Farrar, Straus, and Giroux, 2009),166

against Nakayama's orders. The Filipino men were beheaded, shot, and bayoneted by the Pantingan river.[171] Pedro Felix, a survivor of the massacre, was able to crawl out of the river after four bayonet stabbings and escaped to later testify against the Japanese perpetrators.[172]

Throughout the 65 mile march from Bataan to the POW camp, Camp O' Donnell, the prisoners were given little to no food and water, and consequently many men died of starvation and dehydration. The American and Filipino captives were already weakened from starvation and fighting by the time of their capture and were forced to constantly march without any moment to sleep, urinate, or defecate. The simple rule became clear: if you stopped during the march, you would be beaten or killed. While marching, the American and Filipino captives endured physical abuse, suffering random beatings and bayonet stabbings by their Japanese captors. Men were hit with bamboo poles and rifle butts as they trudged along the road filled with corpses of men who had died. Japanese trucks drove over marchers who collapsed from fatigue and crews were instructed to kill prisoners too weak to continue on. Forced to walk under intense sunlight and in scorching heat for miles on end, the prisoners had no head protection and at times, were forced to sit naked or within sight of water. Other Japanese efforts to psychologically and physically torment their captives included dragging POWs by the neck with a rope behind trucks, pouring out water from prisoners' canteens out of spite, and killing prisoners when they asked for water or desperately tried to drink muddy water from the side of the road. Pausing to help your fellow comrades would endanger your own life, as many survivors who recall the Death March commented on the tor-

---

[171] Norman and Norman, *Tears in the Darkness: The Story of the Bataan Death March and its aftermath,* 202-14.
[172] Norman and Norman, *Tears in the Darkness: The Story of the Bataan Death March and its aftermath,* 202-205.

ment of watching their friends die. Prisoners were ordered by Japanese guards to dig graves for their severely weakened fellow captives, and were shot when refused to comply.

The extreme hunger and thirst would drive some of the American and Filipino soldiers mad. Some prisoners already contracted diseases such as malaria and dysentery, making the relief of water a necessity. Lester Tenney, an American soldier who survived the Bataan Death March, remembers a particular instance of Japanese brutality, during which several prisoners desperate for water, ran towards a carabao wallow for relief. The Japanese guards allowed this, but after the prisoners returned back to line, the Japanese officer, with a "big broad smile" began to search for men with water soaked clothes and ordered the guards to line them up and shoot the several men. Filipino bystanders would attempt to give the marching POWs food and water, by throwing rice cakes and sugar canes. The food saved many soldiers from starvation, but if caught, both the Filipino sympathizer and prisoner would be beaten or killed by Japanese guards.[173]

After reaching Palanga, the first stop towards Camp O'Donnell, prisoners continually died of diseases that spread rampantly. The Japanese did not provide any medical care leaving it up to American medical personnel to tend to the sick with no medical supplies. At the San Fernando trailhead, prisoners were stuffed in overcrowded, hot metal cars on a train towards Capas. Due to the overcrowding, where about 100 men were forced to stand in a boxcar designed to only fit 30-40 men, prisoners died of heat exhaustion and suffocation.[174] Richard Gordon, a Lieutenant from the all American 31st Infantry Regiment, remembers the haunting experience, "Men died standing up, and had no room to fall down." [175]

---

[173] Department of National Defense Philippine Veterans Affairs Office. *Legacy of Heroes: The Story of Bataan and Corregidor*, Directed by Butch Nolasco, https://www.youtube.com/watch?v=ennb2ihsTR8
[174] National Museum of the Air Force. "Bataan Death March."
[175] Department of National Defense Philippine Veterans Affairs Office. *Legacy of*

Upon arriving at Capas, the prisoners were forced to walk a final nine miles to Camp O'Donnell where American and Filipino prisoners continued to die at rates of several hundreds a day. By the time the survivors reached the prisoner camps after 65 miles of torture, all the remaining soldiers had left was their sheer will to survive. The casualty estimates of the Death March range from 7,000-10,000 Filipino deaths and 500-650 American deaths.[176] Of the 70,000 troops that surrendered, only 7,500 would survive.[177] The terrible atrocities suffered by the Filipino and American men may have been influenced by the Japanese *bushido* code. The Japanese highly emphasized that it was cowardly of a soldier to become a prisoner of war, the loyal soldier would save a last bullet for himself, rather than become captured by the enemy. [178]

Surviving the death march was only the first hurdle, for the men that survived, torturous conditions awaited them in prisoner of war camps.

Heroes: The Story of Bataan and Corregidor.
[176] Chun, *The Fall of the Philippines 1941-1942*, 77
[177] Peter Li, *The Search for Justice: Japanese War Crimes*, (New Brunswick, Transaction Publishers, 2003), 81.
[178] David Powers, "Japan: No Surrender in World War Two," *BBC,* Last Modified February 17 2012, Last Accessed August 3, 2017. http://www.bbc.co.uk/history/worldwars/wwtwo/japan_no_surrender_01.shtml

American soldiers carry two off their fellow men to bury at Camp O'Donnell.[179]

Japanese guards forced Filipino citizens to see the murdered POWs. Filipino sympathy towards the POWs did not go unpunished.[180]

---

[179] National Museum of the Air Force. "Bataan Death March."
[180] National Museum of the Air Force. "Bataan Death March."

Men carry those who died during the Death March to be buried.[181]

Survivor Testimonies

There is little record of survivor testimonies or information regarding the Filipino survivors of the Bataan Death March and POW camps. A majority of the information available is often about the American survivors, and although their contributions and experiences should not be ignored, it is equally as important to remember the many Filipinos who also endured the same hardships and sacrifices. This unequal portrayal promotes an image of only Japanese fighting Americans when in reality a large portion of Allied troops that fought in the Philippines were Filipinos.

Specific instances of Japanese cruelty towards the Filipinos include the Pantigan Massacre, as mentioned before.[182] The Japanese also exacted revenge on the Philippine Scouts for their "mauling" of Japanese soldiers during the battle before. The Scouts were excellent marksmen and were picked

---

[181] National Museum of the Air Force. "Bataan Death March."
[182] John Costello, *The Pacific War: 1941-1945* (Atlantic Communications, 1981), 228

out by Japanese who would inspect Filipino POWs' trigger fingers. If found, the Filipino Scout would be beaten.[183] At Camp O'Donnell, the Filipinos would die at the same rate of the Americans. But due to the greater numbers of captured Filipinos, six Filipinos died for every American.[184]

Philippine Scout Lorenzo Apilado

Lorenzo Apilado joined the Philippine Scouts and was assigned to field artillery. During the attack on Lingayen Gulf, Apilado almost died after a bomb landed near his bunk as he was sleeping. During the Death March, Apilado was called out to carry a Japanese soldier's rucksack. While walking over dead bodies of those who had fallen during the horrid march, the Japanese soldiers were kind to give him water. Remarkably, the soldiers let him and his fellow captives free at the town of Pampanga. Apilado would return home, before succumbing to malaria.[185]

Sergeant Atilano David

"I have nightmares around December", Atilano David remarks during an interview with Batilang America News.

---

[183] Norman, *Tears in the darkness*, 185.
[184] Norman, *Tears in the darkness*, 240.
[185] Laureen Diephof, "Lorenzo Apilado, 100, Defied the Death March and malaria," *The Californian*, Last Modified August 3, 2017, Last Accessed August 3, 2017. http://www.thecalifornian.com/story/life/2017/08/04/lorenzo-apilado-defied-bataan-death-march-malaria/104276172/

At only nineteen, Atilano David was enlisted in the Philippine Army and forced to walk during the Death March of Bataan, which took him seven to ten days. A young member of the 31st regiment of the Philippine Division, he recounts his horrifying experience during the Death March including sharing a single tin of jelly and four crackers with three other fellow soldiers. David's account of the Death March inspired him to write about his experience in his book, "End of the Trail: A Novel of the Philippines During World War II".[186]

Elias Coloma

Coloma was a Filipino soldier during the Battle of Bataan and in an interview with the Orange County Register recalls the desperation he and his fellow soldiers felt before the American surrender. Coloma details his death march experience; remembering the brutality of the Japanese guards who would sometimes shoot men through the mouth if asked for water. His willpower to live and return home one day allowed him to continue on. Fortunately, a Filipino civilian miraculously helped him escape while being transferred between prisoner camps. After his escape, Coloma joined the local guerrilla efforts[187].

---

[186] Bev Llorente, "Bataan Death March Survivor Recalls Terrifying Experience," *ABS-CBN News*, December 7, 2016. Accessed July 31, 2017. https://www.balitangamerica.tv/bataan-death-march-survivor-recalls-terrifying-experience/

[187] Tom Berg, "Death March survivor finally tells story," *Orange County Register*, May 17, 2012. Accessed July 31, 2017. http://www.ocregister.com/2012/05/17/death-march-survivor-finally-tells-story/

Hell Ships

The hell ship Oryoku Maru under fire.[188]

The Japanese Imperial Army used ships to transport Allied prisoners of war to meet labor shortages during World War II out of the Philippines. The men lived in cramped conditions with only a small canteen of water and bowl of rice.[189] The ships were unmarked and therefore highly vulnerable to American fire. As a consequence, the U.S. Navy mistakenly sunk five ships carrying 10,000 POWs.

Shinyo Maru held approximately 750 American and Filipino POWs travelling to Manila and was attacked by the US submarine, Paddle, on September 7, 1944. 81 POWs escaped and received help by nearby Filipino guerrillas, while the 667 American and Filipino POWs died in the explosion, by drowning, or were killed by Japanese while attempting to escape.[190] Another hell ship that sunk was the *Oryoku Maru* which held 1,619 Allied POWs along with 1,900 Japanese

---

[188] Lee A. Gladwin, "American POWs on Japanese Ships Take a Voyage into Hell," *U.S. National Archives and Records Administration, Prologue Magazine* Vol. 35, No. 4 (Winter 2003). Last modified July 19, 2017. Accessed August 3, 2017. https://www.archives.gov/publications/prologue/2003/winter/hell-ships-1.html

[189] Ibid.

[190] "Shinyo Maru," Wrecksite. Accessed August 3, 2017. http://www.wrecksite.eu/wreck.aspx?59632, https://www.archives.gov/publications/prologue/2003/winter/hell-ships-1.html

civilians and military personnel. The US Navy attacked the unmarked ship on December 15, 1944. Similar to *Shinyo Maru*, prisoners were shot while trying to escape. Only 403 of the original 1,619 POWs were eventually sent to prisoner camps.[191]

Prisoner of War Camps

The Japanese set up various prisoner of war camps in the Philippines to hold captured American and Filipino soldiers. Most if not all POW camps were primitive, prisoners never received the necessary medical treatment or food and water they needed. As a result, prisoners died at alarming rates; up to 500 men died each day.[192] Mass graves were built right outside the prisoner camps with little covering, revealing decaying flesh every time it rained. The American and Filipino prisoners lived in extremely unsanitary conditions and suffered from malnutrition; the lack of food only accelerated the prisoners' illnesses.

The final destination of Filipino and American POWs following the Death march of Bataan was Camp O'Donnell, where Filipinos and Americans were housed separately. Between April and June of 1942, 1,500 Americans and 20,000 Filipinos died at Camp O'Donnell.[193] American POWs were shipped to POW camps such as Cabanatuan, where able prisoners embarked onto labor camps elsewhere in the Japanese empire. Another prison was the Bilibid prison in Manila; originally an old Spanish prison, reopened by the Japanese to

---

[191] "The Oryoku Maru Story," *Oryoku Maru Online*, Last Modified 1983, Last Accessed July 30, 2017. http://www.oryokumaruonline.org/oryoku_maru_story.html

[192] Department of National Defense Philippine Veterans Affairs Office. *Legacy of Heroes: The Story of Bataan and Corregidor*.

[193] History Channel. *Shootout: Raid on Bataan Death Camp*. Directed by Louis C. Tarantino. 2006. https://www.youtube.com/watch?v=YY9V7vPK5-8.

serve as a transit station and hospital for the captives.[194] Other notable prisoner camps include the Cabanatuan Camp, Los Banos, and Santo Tomas Internment Camp.[195] These camps would be liberated in brave attempts by Americans and Filipinos with MacArthur's return to the islands.

Despite the dire conditions of the prisoners, there were instances of kindness among the sufferers. One particular story was Filipino Sergeant Salvador Floresca's act of generosity. The Sergeant escaped towards the Malinta Tunnel with empty canteens to fill up water for his comrades. Floresca risked his life to retrieve the water as he stumbled over dead soldiers in the dark to a water pipe about half a kilometer away.

Slave Labor

The POWs who would survive the Hell Ships were forced to work slave labor in Japan at mines, factories, and docks. Companies such as Mitsubishi Materials Corporation used American, Filipino, as well as Chinese and British POWs in mining operations. Rabbi Abraham Cooper of the Wiesenthal Center, estimates a total of 12,000 prisoners forced to work, of which 1,100 died.[196] Filipinos were also forced to work during the wartime in mines and plantations for Japanese companies including Mitsui, Mitsubishi, and Nippon Steel. The company, Mitsui Kozan, allegedly used 1.5 million

---

[194] Val Burgess, "Billibid Prison," *Wars' Voices Are you Listening?*, July 12, 2014, accessed August 3, 2017, http://www.warsvoices.org/location/bilibid-prison/

[195] Val Burgess, "Santa Tomas Camp." *Wars' Voices Are you Listening?*, August 1, 2014, accessed August 3, 2017, http://www.warsvoices.org/location/santa-tomas-manilla-luzon/

[196] Will Ripley, "Mitsubishi apologizes to WWII Japanese prisoners of war," *CNN*, July 20, 2015, accessed August 3, 2017, http://www.cnn.com/2015/07/19/asia/mitsubishi-japan-pow-apology/index.html

Scott Neuman, "Japan's Mitsubishi Apologizes For Using U.S. POWs As Forced Labor In WWII", *NPR*, July 19, 2015, accessed August 3, 2017. http://www.npr.org/sections/thetwo-way/2015/07/19/424408003/japans-mitsubishi-to-apologize-for-using-u-s-pows-as-laborers-in-wwii

Filipino workers to work in a copper mine under life-threatening conditions.[197] It is not until recently that the Filipino victims and American POWs have been successful in attaining reparations and compensations.

During the Japanese campaign and conquest of the Philippines, many Filipino civilians endured the brunt of the atrocities committed. Similar to the Asian countries the Japanese had previously conquered during the war, the Japanese military raped, abducted, and killed numbers of Filipina women and men. The Japanese established comfort stations throughout the Philippines during its occupation, including Manila, Northern Luzon, and Leyte. Many women were forcibly kidnapped at home or while running errands. They were taken to Japanese garrisons or military camps to be raped, some multiple times a week, and some even multiple times a day.[198] The Filipina victims were hardly adults, most only 13 to 15 years old. More than 1,000 girls were comfort women according to researchers' estimates.[199]

Many Filipina comfort women's stories are similar to that of Hilaria Bustamante, who was abducted while walking by three Japanese soldiers at the age of 16. She was taken to a garrison where she cooked and washed clothing during the day and was raped by several soldiers during the night for fifteen gruesome months.[200] The Filipina comfort women are

---

[197] The Associated Press, "Wartime Workers in the Philippines to Sue Japanese Companies," *The New York Times*, March 27, 2000, accessed July 27, 2017. http://www.nytimes.com/2000/03/27/world/wartime-workers-in-the-philippines-to-sue-japanese-companies.html?mcubz=1

[198] "An Evaluative Research in the Implementation of Assistance to Lolas of Crisis (ALCS) Project, *Department of Social Welfare and Development and the Asian Women's Fund*, Last accessed August 2, 2017. http://www.awf.or.jp/pdf/ALCS.pdf http://www.awf.or.jp/e1/philippine-00.html

[199] Dominque Mosbergen, "The Harrowing Story of Filipina Women Enslaved in Japan's Wartime Rape Camps," *The Huffington Post*, Last Modified May 18, 2016, Last Accessed August 3, 2017. http://www.huffingtonpost.com/entry/comfort-women-philippines-m-evelina-galang_us_57232d48e4b0f-309baf08490

[200] Floyd Whaley, "In Philippines, World War II's Lesser Known Sex Slaves Speak

not as known because of their lesser numbers as compared to the comfort women of Korea and China, and their sufferings have yet to be acknowledged by the Japanese government.

Out," *The New York Times,* Last Modified January 29, 2016, Last Accessed August 3, 2017.
https://www.nytimes.com/2016/01/30/world/asia/japan-philippines-comfort-women-emperor-akihito.html

CHAPTER 5
The Female Faces of the Philippine Guerrillas

A Young Filipina Guerrilla posing with a USAFFE Tarlac Flag to mark the success of the guerrillas and American units retaking Tarlac Province from the Japanese, August 1945.[201]

---

[201] "Greatest Generation Tumblr, "Bag of Dirt: A Young Filipino Resistance Fighter," *Greatest Generation Tumblr: Our Grandparents Were Heroes Once, The National World War II Museum, New Orleans*, Last Accessed July 10th, 2017, https://www.pinterest.com/pin/310115124312465095.

Women, similar to the ethnic minorities who served as guerrillas throughout the war, are less well known for their military services during the war. Women's history during World War II relates moreso to their participation and aid in relation to their roles in working in military based industries (i.e. Rosie the Riveter) on America's domestic front or as nurses (in association with the Red Cross) as noted in common American histories of World War II. What makes the Underground Resistance so unique in the Philippines are the numerous accounts of female led insurgencies during the Japanese Occupation. Equal to men in both combat and strategy, these Filipina women broke gender conventions, organized guerrilla units in expansive territories/terrain, and conducted much of the spy and infiltration work to provide stable communication and supply networks in which the Underground Resistance used throughout the war.

Many scholarly sources such as Evelyn M. Monahan's and Rosemary Neidel-Greenlee's *All this Hell: U.S. Nurses Imprisoned by the Japanese* or Elizabeth M. Normon's *We Band of Angels* highlight the brave lives of the American women captured by the Japanese army who were forced to live in the squalid POW and internment camps of Luzon. Other detailed narratives of the female war experience are those of the American and European women, like Margaret Utinsky and Claire Phillips, who helped maintain spy and supply networks to the underground resistance and guerrillas that fought off the Japanese.[202] Many of these American women's experiences and efforts further add to the guerrilla narrative as to just how socially inclusive the Philippine underground resistance was.

---

[202] Bataan Diary, "Introducing Bataan," *Bataan Diary*, Last Modified December 2, 2010, Last Accessed July 8th, 2017, http://www.bataandiary.com/Introducing.htm.

1943 American propaganda poster rallying Americans to help in the war efforts so as to help liberate American nurses and civilians from the POW and internment camps of the Philippines.[203]

But, similar to the ethnic minorities who served as guerrillas in the cordilleras of Luzon, the Filipina guerrilla experience tends to be harder to locate. As female guerrillas, Filipinas represented double minorities (women that are marginalized by both their race and gender). This form of marginalization resulted in the lack of properly recorded

---

[203] "Bataan Angels 1943 World War II Poster," 2008-12-22 22:41 Ksibley 374×500× (190232 bytes) *{{Information |Description=US Government Poster |Source=Ben Perry, Nov. 21, 2008, hellobp@gmail.com |Date=1943 |Author=US Government |Permission= |other_versions= }}*

recognition by military personnel. These professional missteps have unfortunately dampened the critical roles women played in the war as nurses, doctors, soldiers, commanders, spies, and above all, as guerrilla fighters.

Although both Philippine men and women throughout the war received heavy scrutiny, maltreatment, torture, and suspicion by the Japanese officers who oversaw civilian activities, women suffered other intense fears and forms of assault from Japanese overseers. Wartime presents a desperate and immoral landscape. Women in the Philippines, in addition to the general brutalities of war, faced additional threats stemming specifically from the traditional assumptions as to the weakness associated with gender. Women and children throughout many of the world's histories of conquest have experienced similar horrors of rape, molestation, torture, physical and psychological abuse, and enslavement.[204] The women of the Pacific Theater were forced under terrifying circumstances to obey the Japanese invaders or suffer the mentioned consequences of war. Despite the atrocities committed against Filipinas by the Japanese Imperial Army, Filipinas fought alongside their male counterparts as guerrillas and leaders of resistance despite the risks.

---

[204] Margaret D. Stetz & Bonnie B. C. Oh, *Legacies of the Comfort Women of World War II* (New York: Routledge, 2015), xii, 98.

Filipina Perspectives

Valeria 'Yay' Panlilio

Cry Freedom is a post war film starring Filipino actors Pancho Magalona and Rosa Rosal depicting the contributions of the Marking's Guerrillas highlighting the real life love story between its guerrilla leaders Yay Panlilio and Marcos V. Augustin.[205]

---

[205] Video 48, "The Fifties #618 Pancho Magalona and Rosa Rosal in Lamberto V. Avellana's "Cry Freedom" 1959," Last Modified April 22nd, 2014, Last Accessed August 1st, 2017, http://video48.blogspot.com/2014/04/the-fifties-618-pancho-magalona-and.html.

Valeria Panlilio was a famous Filipino-American journalist. Raised in Colorado, Valeria, or better known by her peers as "Yay", returned to the Philippines prior to World War II with her first husband, Eduardo Panlilio, to start a new life surrounded by her native Philippine culture.[206] But within years of returning to the Philippines, she parted ways with her husband and began to write as a professional journalist for the newspaper *The Philippines Herald* in Manila. Soon, as war seemed imminent in the Pacific, Yay joined the United States Army Intelligence Agency. Once affiliated with the American military, she met another determined passionate soldier bent on liberating the Philippines from the threat of Japanese imperialism.[207] This soldier was Marcos V. Agustin. Yay and Agustin would eventually fall in love during the war and both head the famous guerrilla organization known as Marking's Guerrillas.

Yay would go on to become a guerrilla army colonel for Marking's Guerrillas. In her autobiography, *The Crucible: An Autobiography by Colonel Yay, Filipina American Guerrilla*, Yay describes the atrocities of the war, her purpose and determination despite the lows and hopelessness of her men, and her romance with Agustin despite their circumstances. Histories written on Yay including her own biography paint her as a mother figure to her despairing guerrillas who often questioned their abilities in winning the war, defending their loved ones, and whether or not their hopes on the return of American troops were meaningless.[208] As colonel, she routed out Japanese spies, Filipino traitors (the Makapili), and made sure that their enemies were executed swiftly to avoid both

---

[206] Theresa Kaminski, *Angels of the Underground: The American Women Who Resisted the Japanese in the Philippines in World War II* (New York: Oxford University Press, 2016), 29.
[207] Kaminski, *Angels of the Underground*, 240, 241.
[208] Ray C. Hunt & Bernard Norling, *Behind Japanese Lines: An American Guerrilla in the Philippines* (University of Press of Kentucky, 2014), 112-115.

Japanese military police repercussions and so as to exact justice discreetly. She was known to try and uphold the codes of conduct in her unit including avoiding the temptation to kill the enemy brutally and inhumanely as the Japanese were described in doing to her Filipina and Filipino peers.[209]

Among her many other contributions to the underground resistance, includes her skills as a journalist and orator. During the Bataan ordeal, Yay served as a radio talk show host who was forced to deliver Japanese propaganda.[210] In between the lines she was forced to read, she cleverly squeezed in phrases and words that would hint to the Philippine listeners to remain steadfast to rebelling against the Japanese forces.[211] To avoid being caught by the Japanese, Yay escaped out of Manila and found her way to Marking's Guerrilla camp.

Yay's other contribution to Filipina History is her honesty in her depictions concerning the brutalities of war. She describes in her autobiography and in correspondences the rivalries felt and displayed amongst the Filipino guerrillas, the rape and innocent killing committed by both sides of the war, the visual horrors of decimated villages and cities, and the desperateness of total war that fuel people's' immoral actions when seeking to survive.[212] The respect she gained, despite the disposition historically and culturally placed on her gender, from her male peers say much about her courage as a Filipina soldier, leader, and intellectual.

Josefa Capistrano

Another brave young resistance fighter in a field of her own is Josefa Capistrano. Capistrano founded the Philip-

---

[209] Hunt & Norling, *Behind Japanese Lines*, 128.
[210] Kaminski, *Angels of the Underground*, 99-101.
[211] Ronald D. Klein, *The Other Empire: The Literary Views of Japan from the Philippines, Singapore, and Malaysia* (Quezon City: The University of the Philippines Press, 2008), 107, 108.
[212] Hunt & Norling, *Behind Japanese Lines*, 128-131.

pines' first Women's Auxiliary Service (WAS) in Mindanao. A Filipina-Chinese mestiza who was born to a family with prestigious political ties, Capistrano, similar to Yay, was a free thinking Filipina ahead of her time. She strove to train and establish a purely female unit that would be recognized as an official unit of the Philippines Military.[213] The performance and skill of the WAS served as just one of the many landmark advances in women's rights and social presence in Modern Philippines' History. Capistrano would continue to argue after the war for her unit's recognition as an official entity of the Philippine Army leading her WAS to become recognized by the Philippine Military Armed Forces after the war. It would be renamed the Women's Auxiliary Corps in 1963.[214]

Capistrano's WAS numbered to 3,000 militarily trained women skilled in combat, small industries (making bullets, textiles, bandages), nursing, and handling covert operations, particularly as spies, for both the American Allies and the Filipino guerrilla networks.[215] Her female guerrillas successfully worked alongside Wendell Fertig's guerrillas in Mindanao throughout the war thus proving that women could match men in battle and in their patriotism.

---

[213] Keats, *They Fought Alone*, 221, 245.
[214] William B. Depasupil, "Women's Auxiliary Corps Unmanned After 50 Years," *The Manila Times*, Last Modified July 5th, 2013, Last Accessed August 2nd, 2017, http://www.manilatimes.net/womens-auxiliary-corps-unmanned-after-50-years/16088/.
[215] Evelyn Mallillin Jamboy, *The Resistance Movement in Lanao, 1942-1945* (Coordination Center of Research and Development MSU-Iligan Institute of Technology, 2006), 74.

A training still of the Filipina Women's Auxiliary Service (WAS) founded by Josefa Capistrano in Mindanao. These women were the first group of Filipinas to train and serve as combat guerrillas, November 8th, 1941.[216]

Nieves Fernandez

Captain Nieves Fernandez showing a fellow soldier, U.S. Army Pvt. Andrew Lupiba, her techniques in executing Japanese soldiers effectively as a guerrilla fighter. Photographed November 1944.[217]

---

[216] https://www.pinterest.com/historyspam66/phillipines-soldiers-civilians-and-battles/.

[217] FMA Academy, "International Women's Day - Nieves Fernandez," *Filipino*

Nieves Fernandez is one of the lesser known Filipina guerrilla leaders. She is recorded by her peers and the local communities of Tacloban on the island of Leyte, as a simple Filipina school teacher who defended her homelands from the imperialist Japanese forces the moment her students were threatened to be taken away by Japanese soldiers.[218] She was a skilled marksman and bolo fighter. Fernandez would gain the respect of native locals, lead men into battle, and was so successful in taking out Japanese patrols that the Japanese military stationed in the city, Tacloban, placed a 10,000 peso bounty on her head.[219] Fernandez like many other guerrillas throughout the Philippines relied on makeshift weapons such as the "paltik" (a homemade shotgun made of gas pipes), bolos, homemade grenades (casings filled with old nails) and whatever items her 110 manned guerrilla unit could pilfer from the Japanese.[220] Fernandez would live to be in her early nineties residing in Tacloban and would be survived by her sons and grandchildren. The only evidence of her heroics that survive remain in one photo (as displayed previously) and through a small 1944 American newspaper article depicting her guerrilla contributions prior to the arrival of MacArthur at Leyte.[221]

Martial Arts Academy: Certified and Comprehensive Instruction in the Filipino Martial Arts, Last Modified March 8th, 2016, Last Accessed August 4th, 2017, http://fmaacademy.com/tag/captain-nieves/.

[218] FMA Academy, "International Women's Day - Nieves Fernandez."
[219] Marc V., "14 Amazing Fillipina Heroines You Don't Know But You Should," *Filipiknow,* Last Modified July 27th, 2014, Last Accessed August 4th, 2017, http://www.filipiknow.net/greatest-filipina-heroines/.
[220] Michael Sellers, "Captain Nieves Fernandez - WWII Guerrilla Leader in Leyte, Philippines," Last Modified February 11th, 2017, Last Accessed August 4th, 2017, http://www.michaeldsellers.com/blog/2017/02/11/looking-for-info-on-captain-nieves-fernandez-wwii-guerrilla-leader-in-leyte-philippines/.
[221] Unknown Author, "School Ma'am Led Guerrillas On Leyte," *Lewiston Daily Sun,* October 26th, 1944, Last Accessed August 4th, 2017, http://www.michaeldsellers.com/blog/2017/02/11/looking-for-info-on-captain-nieves-fernandez-wwii-guerrilla-leader-in-leyte-philippines/.

Leading Women Among the Huks

Felipa Culala

Felipa Culala, known more commonly by her peers as Dayang-Dayang (a name attributed to a famous Moro princess), was one of the four co-founders of the Huk organization in 1942 after the execution of its first leader, Crisanto Evangelista.[222] She served as the only active woman to be elected to the Hukbalahap Military Committee acting as the head of the Huk guerrilla units of the East Pampanga District in Luzon.[223] Similar to other guerrilla women of her calibre, Culala was known for making do with what little resources and manpower she had especially in the lesser known Battle of Mandili. In this event, Culala staged an ambush to rescue her captured guerrilla soldiers from within the Japanese holding of the barrio of Mandili (Culala's hometown) and with less than 140 men, was able to eliminate 40 Japanese officers, 68 police officers, and pilfered the remaining Japanese resources from the battle for the Huk guerrillas.[224] Culala would prove to be a a great military leader and strategist but would experience a great deal of scrutiny amongst her male Huk peers.

Recent resources pertaining to Felipa's actions as a member of the Huk committee would paint her in two radically different depictions: one as a strong leader who had a commanding presence or as a flaunting, conceited, and pow-

---

[222] Alfred W. McCoy, ed., *An Anarchy of Families: State and Family in the Philippines* (Madison: The University of Wisconsin Press, 2009), 62-65.

[223] Tonette Orejas, "Last Living Woman Huk Leader Gets Pension," *Inquirer.Net*, Last Modified June 24th, 2014, Last Accessed August 4th, 2017, http://newsinfo.inquirer.net/613833/last-living-woman-huk-leader-gets-pension-back.

[224] Leonard Davis, *Revolutionary Struggle in the Philippines* (New York: Palgrave Macmillan Press, 1989), 37.

er hungry woman who did not heed the Huk rules of conduct.[225] It would be the latter depiction that would define Culala leading to a trial and her execution by firing squad for her unwanted "behavior" that labeled her as a detriment to the Huk guerrilla operations.[226] Huk women after the war argued that Culala was simply a threat to the prominence of her male peers, especially Taruc, and the party found means of proving Culala's inability to lead or have a significant role in the Huk resistance.[227] These discrepancies in narrative as to the true personality of Culala point to a clear issue predominantly pertaining to the gender hierarchies and the patriarchal culture of the time period. The difficulty in finding solid resources on Culala, along with the surviving depictions of Culala that focus on her negative characteristics attributed directly to her gender, taken together reveal the harsh barriers of discrimination that women, Filipina guerrillas, faced in their goals of liberating the Philippines from the Japanese Imperial Army.

Other Huk women who served as guerrillas during World War II include Celia Mariano-Pomeroy, Simeona Punsalan-Tapang, and Elena Poblete also known as Kumander Mameng, daughter of Huk co-founder Bernardo Poblete. Poblete was known to serve on the frontlines and was recorded to have died in battle among the male Huks she led.[228] The Huk guerrilla force throughout its existence during the war would have a substantial amount of female recruits that would contribute equal efforts to the resistance movement as

---

[225] Davis, *Revolutionary Struggle in the Philippines*, 37.
[226] Marc V., "14 Amazing Fillipina Heroines You Don't Know But You Should."
[227] Cynthia G. Franklin, Ruth Hsu, & Suzanne Kosanke, ed., *Navigating Island and Continents: Conversations and Contestations in and Around the Pacific, Selected Essays, Vol. 17* (Honolulu: Colleges of Languages, Linguistics and Literature, University of Hawai'i, 2000), 8.
[228] Tonette Orejas, "Last Living Woman Huk Leader Gets Pension," *Inquirer.Net*, Last Modified June 24th, 2014, Last Accessed August 4th, 2017, http://newsinfo.inquirer.net/613833/last-living-woman-huk-leader-gets-pension-back.

their male Huk peers. The surviving historical resources on Filipinas in the resistance prove that the guerrilla movement served as an opportunity and platform for Filipinas to join the war effort and break out of the traditional social expectations placed upon Southeast Asian women.

Maria Rosa Henson

Maria Rosa Henson would represent and experience the worst of Japanese military atrocities inflicted upon Filipinas throughout the war. Henson's experience as both a female guerrilla and comfort woman highlights the risks and ultimate vulnerabilities that women experienced in the Pacific under Japanese occupation. Women throughout the Pacific had heard the rumors and seen the atrocities exacted on Asian women by Japanese soldiers. Rape, abduction, mutilation, executions, and murder were daily threats that Filipina women faced.[229] As a Filipino girl growing up during the war, simple tasks like getting water or picking up goods such as groceries for one's family in the province, or small towns, came to be known as dangerous opportunities for women to be taken advantage of by Japanese soldiers.[230]

Regardless of age, class, or occupation, Filipina women like other Asian women throughout the Japanese occupied Pacific were susceptible to sexual assaults. Henson, at the age of 15 was repeatedly raped by Japanese soldiers in her hometown Pasay prior to joining the Hukbalahap resistance.[231] En-

---

[229] Wallace Edwards, *Comfort Women: A History of Japanese Forced Prostitution During the Second World War* (Absolute Crime, 2013), Kindle, Introduction.
[230] Wallace Edwards, *Comfort Women: A History of Japanese Forced Prostitution During the Second World War* (Absolute Crime, 2013), Kindle, Introduction, Chapter 1.
[231] Maria Rosa Henson, *Comfort Woman: A Filipina's Story of Prostitution and Slavery Under the Japanese Military* (New York: Rowman & Littlefied, 2017), 29.

raged by the actions and invasion of her body and home by the Japanese Imperial Army, Henson would relay reconnaissance information for the Huks until her capture and arrest in 1943 in the suburbs of Angeles.[232] As a captured guerrilla, her body was taken advantage of again by Japanese soldiers and she became a comfort woman. Even as a comfort woman, Henson would still try to help her Philippine people and when given the opportunity to speak with a local at one of the fences where she was imprisoned, was able to relay information to a Filipino villager of the oncoming Japanese encroachment and raids to the area.[233]

Henson along with her accomplishments would continue to serve her country after the war and was one of the first Southeast Asian women to speak out about the Japanese abuse of the women they captured and molested throughout the Pacific Theater. Henson's roles as a female guerrilla, comfort woman, and women's activist further promote both the diversity and adversity the underground resistance encompassed and its lasting legacy on its promotion of civil liberties and humanitarianism long after the conclusion of the war.

---

[232] Henson, *Comfort Woman*, 37-59.

[233] Kathryn J. Atwood, *Women Heroes of World War II: The Pacific Theater, 15 Stories of Resistance, rescue, Sabotage, and Survival* (Chicago: Chicago Review Press Incorporated, 2017), 105.

[235]*Actress Carmen Rosales in her film Guerilyera (1946) directed by Octavio Silos. Rosales' character in the film was a female guerrilla fighting off Japanese forces.[234] Carmen Rosales was a famous mestiza actress who also served as a guerrilla fighter after the death of her husband at the hands of Japanese soldiers.[235]*

Filipina Guerrillas and their Retellings of their Roles as Guerrillas: Contributions to Filipina-American History

Many Filipinas after the war immigrated to the United States to start a new life after their devastating experiences of death, sexual assault, and all the brutalities associated with the Pacific War. The United States appeared to be an amica-

---

[234] Danny Dolor "Carmen Rosales as Guerilyera," *The Philippine Star*, Last Modified June 14th, 2015, Last Accessed August 5th, 2017, https://www.pressreader.com/philippines/the-philippine-star/20150614/282402693010462.

[235] Ernie Pecho, "Carmen Rosales Movie Queen and War Heroine," *Philippine Daily Inquirer*, March 13th, 2005, Last Accessed August 5th, 2017.

ble environment to begin a new life considering the World War II Allied relationship, collaboration in the liberation of the Philippines, and because of America's imperialist legacy of acculturating the Philippine peoples to the West. Filipina women like the late Dorothy Dore Dowlen would immigrate to the United States from the island of Mindanao. She, like many after the war, brought with her a desolate experience of World War II from of the female perspective rife with the heavy memories of the violent deaths of honorable loved ones and guerrilla resistance fighters. Dowlen herself humbly served as a trained medical aide under USAFFE whose experiences included her family being torn apart by Japanese bombardment, her first husband killed for his efforts and connections with resistance fighters, and the wrecking and uprooting of her homeland, family, and way of life.[236] The lives of Philippine immigrant women therefore represent valuable resources, and honorary mentions, to the many faces that contributed to the underground resistance and liberation of the Philippines. Their migration and settlement in the United States highlight their insurmountable vigor long after the hurdles of World War II.

Lourdes Poblete

Lourdes Poblete is living proof as to the major contributions that Filipina women made to the underground resistance movement. The daughter of a Filipino-American military officer, Poblete and her siblings were raised on and around American military base environments like Fort Mckinley located near Pasig City on the island of Luzonn. It would be Poblete's family ties to the American military that would allow for her to receive an education and strong grasp

---

[236] Dorothy Dore Dowlen, *Enduring What Cannot Be Endured: Memoir of a Woman Medical Aide in the Philippines in World War II* (McFarland & Company, Inc., Publishers, 2001), 5, 9, 30-36, 116, 131.

of the English language which would aid her in her efforts as a Luzon guerrilla.

With the 1941 invasion of the Japanese Imperial Army, her father, who was still employed by the American military would be forced to endure the Bataan Death March, leaving Poblete and her family to find various means of survival. Poblete's mother would conduct small domestic industries (sewing and textile work). Poblete herself would take long treks, often times by bancas, to gather local produce and sell whatever food supplies were left once the Japanese Imperial Army would take their share of the locals' harvested goods. With over six mouths to feed in one household, Poblete and her family's subsistence living represent just one example of the ever tiring daily workloads Philippine families would face in war time as the Japanese presence manipulated the Philippines' economy and resources.

Poblete like many of the brave Filipina women previously mentioned felt an obligation to help her fellow countrymen, liberate her country from Japanese armed forces, and protect her family. She joined the guerrilla movement as a teenager under the 10th Military District's Live or Die Unit.[237] As directed by her commanding guerrilla officer, Captain Julian Alvarez, Poblete's many missions included delivering propaganda (newspapers in particular) to specific guerrilla conspirators.

Poblete, like other guerrilla insurgents, had to always remain weary of those around her. She made sure not to provide any hints of her whereabouts, her affiliations, and was keen on conversing with only those who made sure to say specific code words or statements that would insure their conversation was guerrilla organized. Poblete's experience

---

[237] Manzel Delacruz, "The Women Behind the Bataan Legacy Project," *Positively Filipino: Your Window on the Filipino Diaspora*, Last Modified April 5th, 2017, Last Accessed August 5th, 2017, http://www.positivelyfilipino.com/magazine/the-women-behind-the-bataan-legacy-project.

as a guerrilla carrier reveals the intense means in which insurgents maintained their forms of security. There were a number of Filipinos who were pro-Japanese often seeking to avoid any harm or harassment from the Japanese occupying forces. The para-military pro-Japanese group, the Makapili, were one such group that believed that the Allies' defeat by the Japanese served as a stepping stone towards the Philippines' independence.[238] Filipino spies for the Japanese could easily pose as guerrilla recruits and often tried to join the resistance as fresh recruits in order to provide the Japanese intelligence with information regarding guerrilla networks. Filipino Guerrillas and American soldiers therefore had to provide means of evidence that proved their loyalty to the cause of liberating the Philippines. Either American made goods (Lucky Strike cigarettes) or propaganda supply items that were trademarked by MacArthur (cigarette boxes, newspapers, chocolate, pencils, gum, etc.) with his slogan "I Shall Return."[239] Poblete's propaganda guerrilla missions confirms these historical observations as to the discrete operations of the Philippine guerrillas.

Other tasks given to Poblete included taking on specific jobs assigned to her by her guerrilla liaison, Captain Julian Alvarez, as a regular factory worker for a Japanese manned shipping and distributing company in the Manila region. Her covert mission was to provide reconnaissance as to the details of the Japanese workhouses in the Philippines to her guerrilla commander. The job was very strenuous, forcing her to work long hours lifting shipments. The Japanese

---

[238] Mercedes G. Planta, *"Sakdalistas' Struggle for Philippine Independence,1930-1945,* Review," *Philippine Studies: Historical and Ethnographic Viewpoints* Vol. 63, No. 4 (December 2014): 592-593.

[239] Supreme Commander of the Allied Powers, General Staff of General MacArthur, *Reports of General MacArthur: The Campaigns of MacArthur in the Pacific, Vol. I.* (Library of Congress, 1966), 81 & Bruce Henderson, *Rescue at Los Banos: The Most Daring Prison Camp Raid of World War II* (New York: HarperCollins, 2015), 178.

management were very strict according to Poblete and the workers were told not to talk to other Filipino workers in the facility otherwise would be forced to stand outside in the hot sun for the rest of the day alone.

Lourdes Poblete as a young girl posing with her younger sisters and her parents, photographed in the 1920s. Courtesy of Mrs. Lourdes Catig-Poblete's Personal Collection.[240]

---

[240] Catig-Poblete, Lourdes. *Family Photograph*. 1920s. Lourdes Catig-Poblete Personal Collection, San Francisco.

Poblete would soon be found out for her ties to the guerrilla movement and was taken from her home in Pasig City. Her father had been able to make it back home after the Bataan Death March atrocity. He was unfamiliar with the brutality of the Japanese, thus, her parents were unable to fend off the Japanese soldiers at their door so as not to provoke them from hurting the rest of their household filled with Poblete's younger siblings. The soldiers at the front steps of the Catig household stated that the young Lourdes would return the next day.

"Tomorrow," according to Mrs. Poblete, "became two years."[241]

The next few years would be filled with desperate longings for home, worries that her family might have perished after her abduction, that perhaps the Allies would never liberate the Philippines, if she would be forced to become a comfort woman, or whether or not she would be tortured or killed. Poblete was moved to the infamous Fort Santiago where many suffering POWs and insurgents were kept and killed. In the tunnels of the fort, Poblete would find a kindred spirit in her cell, another fellow guerrilla Filipina by the name of Natividad, or Naty for short. The stench of the sick and suffering Allied POWs would fill the tunnels and remind the two young women as to how desperate and terrifying their situation was. Poblete remembers that her main task with her cellmate was to maintain the cleanliness of the tunnels and to make blackout curtains in preparation for American bombardments of the towns surrounding Manila. The Japanese colonel in charge of the fort made sure that the "cleaning ladies" would not be harmed or sexually assaulted by ordering the Japanese soldiers not to harm the women otherwise they would be decapitated as punishment.

The medical aid afforded the captured POWs and guer-

---

[241] Lourdes Catig-Poblete, Interview by Stacey Anne Baterina Salinas, San Francisco, July 4th, 2017.

rilla insurgents was little to none. Poblete would remark that body lice were a common pain and would line and infest her clothing and nether regions making her chores and simple movements constantly uncomfortable. Showers or baths were rare and a comfortable place to relieve oneself was simply wishful thinking.

As the war raged on and the success of the collaborations between the guerrillas and the Allied forces changed the tide of war to benefit the Allies, Japanese officials at Fort Santiago decided to move the POWs and remaining supplies elsewhere to avoid Allied aerial bombings. Poblete and her cellmate were relocated to an old mansion belonging to one of the prominent old families of Manila, the Aranetas. Placed in the servants' quarters, Poblete and her friend felt blessed to have a restroom, shower, clean running water, and proper beds. But the fear of aerial bombings, raids, friendly fire, and perhaps last minute executions of POWs by fleeing Japanese soldiers ran through the minds of Poblete and her guerrilla comrade.

Confined to one room in a large mansion, escape seemed a possibility to Poblete. The mansion after days became quiet and eventually was deserted. Pobelete and her friend braved the empty halls of the mansion and walked out of the iron gates of the property without a scratch. The two parted ways wishing each other luck and safe travels as they walked from Manila to their neighboring hometowns, Pasig and Pasay.

"My one regret," described Mrs. Poblete, "was that I did not look for her after the war."[242]

Poblete's one day trek to her hometown proved to be a frightening final stretch to her freedom. She feared that contact with any stranger acting as a Makapili along the road could mean terrible repercussions if it was found out as to where she had come from and why.

---

[242] Lourdes Catig-Poblete, Interview by Stacey Anne Baterina Salinas, San Francisco, July 4th, 2017.

Eventually, Poblete would make it to her home, to find her family alive. The only missing smiling face she was expecting to see was that of her younger brother, Ramon, who was abducted by the Japanese Army at the age of 16 and never heard from again.

"That was the loneliest day, I loved my brother. My father said to imagine and pray that he was sent to another province, or escaped, or was let go and was being taken cared of by other Filipino families who might have taken him in, he will come back," Mrs. Poblete recalls.[243]

Poblete would lose another sibling, a younger sibling once the American aerial bombings increased throughout the region of Manila and its neighboring towns. Her younger sister, en route with the rest of the family upon trying to find a secure place to hide, was hit by friendly fire as they made their way through the cemeteries that Filipinos had hoped would be safe zones.

"This is too much for me, not two of my siblings. Lord, why not me instead? Not my sister."[244]

As the guerrillas and Allies became more certain that the liberation of the Philippines was within reach, Poblete too put her skills to good use in helping surviving American and Filipino soldiers recover. Prior to the war, Poblete studied to become a nurse. Poblete near the conclusion of the war worked for the Red Cross for six months and would recruit her high school friends from her hometown to help jumpstart the morale of the war torn men (playing piano, helping write soldiers' letters to be sent home, combing their hair, or providing them with medical relief) and preparing them for the road home once they recovered from their ailments received from the war.

---

[243] Lourdes Catig-Poblete, Interview by Stacey Anne Baterina Salinas, San Francisco, July 4th, 2017.
[244] Lourdes Catig-Poblete, Interview by Stacey Anne Baterina Salinas, San Francisco, July 4th, 2017.

After the war, Poblete would serve as a secretary to Colonel Mitchum in an army hospital while attending courses at the University of Manila. She would also be asked to help in the beginning stages of the war crime trials of the Pacific led by General MacArthur. Poblete would be asked to pinpoint the face of major Japanese officers like Colonel Nakahama, who had spared her and Naty from the sexual assaults of the Fort Santiago Japanese soldiers. During her time in Manila, helping with the tribunal proceedings and attending to her own work, Poblete would meet her husband, a young news reporter by the name of Poblete, whose name she would take. Mr. Augusto Alemani Poblete would interview her for her experiences during the war and would become smitten with her.

After her husband's death, Mrs. Poblete would immigrate to the United States and work at San Francisco General Hospital as a medical worker. Despite her contributions to the underground resistance, like many other guerrilla men and women, she would not be honored for her duties as a guerrilla till 2017. By the acknowledgement of the California State Legislature following President Barack Obama's Filipino Veterans of World War II Congressional Gold Medal Act, Filipino and Filipina guerrilla veterans would finally be recognized for their valor during World War II. On April 8th, 2017, a strong and spirited Mrs. Lourdes Catig-Poblete well into her nineties, finally received her long overdue Congressional Gold Medal.

Conclusion

By the end of the war, it was estimated that for every ten male guerrillas, there was one female guerrilla that participated in the underground resistance.[245] The biographies,

---

[245] Barton C. Hacker & Margaret Vining, ed., *A Companion to Women's Military*

contributions, and details of the few women mentioned in this chapter showcase the risks and limitations that Filipinas faced in their pursuit of a noble cause in liberating the Philippines. Their experiences as women reveal the other horrors of war that pertain specifically to their gender that oftentimes, go unnoticed, or are simply seen as the more typical casualties of war (rape, kidnapping, torture) thus oversimplifying the atrocities and transgressions experienced by women in wartime.

The few primary and secondary resources that highlight the presence of Filipina guerrillas that survive are rare and overlooked, especially in Western literature. The Filipina guerrilla history thus solidifies the need to redress historical narratives of World War II, especially pertaining to the many marginalized communities (based on gender and ethnicity) who contributed to the peace achieved in the Pacific at the conclusion of World War II. Above all, Filipina guerrilla histories most importantly add to the twentieth century landmarks of women's social achievements and their expressions of self empowerment.

> This chapter is especially dedicated to Mrs. Lourdes Catig-Poblete for her dedication, past and present, to the preservation and recognition of Filipino American Women in World War II.

(Boston: Brill, 2012), 267.

A 1945 Los Angeles Examiner headline that argues and approves of the recognition of female guerrilla fighters in the Philippines.[246]

---

[246] QRST, "1945 Headline Newspaper Women Guerrillas Fight in World War II," *Ebay*, Last Accessed July 8th, 2017, http://www.ebay.com/itm/1945-headline-newspaper-WOMEN-GUERRILLA-s-FIGHT-in-WW-II-FRANCE-PHIL-IPPINES-/371991116955?hash=item569c65fc9b.

CHAPTER 6
The Liberation of the Philippines

MacArthur's Return

MacArthur returns ashore the Philippines during the Battle of Leyte.[247]

Throughout the Japanese occupation of the Philippines, Filipino guerilla resistance persisted while Allied efforts regrouped in Australia as MacArthur and his colleagues plotted their next actions. Despite suggestion to attack Japanese

---

[247] Gaetano Faillace,"Douglas MacArthur lands on Leyte,"*National Archives*, Last Modified October 1944, Last Accessed August 1, 2017.https://catalog.archives.gov/id/531424

occupied Formosa instead of the Philippines, MacArthur insisted the Americans had a moral obligation to liberate the 16 million Filipino citizens from Japanese occupation.[248]

Invasion & American Liberation of the Philippines
Battle of Leyte and Leyte Gulf
On October 20th, 1944, "A-day", MacArthur and his forces landed on Leyte with the help of Filipino guerillas who remained in continual communication as American invasion forces approached. Beginning with a four hour bombardment, American forces successfully established their positions on the beachheads. The Japanese were also determined and received reinforcements leading up to one of the largest naval battles in history. The Battle of Leyte Gulf from October 23th to 26th of 1944 decisively resulted in heavy Japanese losses and triumph for MacArthur.[249] The Japanese unleashed a new weapon, kamikaze[250], which impacted some American aircraft carriers, but their efforts were only in vain. The Americans finally made an advance on Ormoc Bay and effectively cut off Japanese resupply of troops to the region. The Battle of Leyte lasted for roughly three months, ending in December. After an estimated 60,000 Japanese deaths and 3,500 American deaths[251], General Yamashita was forced to withdraw closer to Manila.

---

[248] Charles R. Anderson, "Leyte," *U.S. Army Center of Military History*, Last Modified October 3 2003, Last Accessed August 3, 2017. http://www.history.army.mil/brochures/leyte/leyte.htm
[249] Costello, *The Pacific War: 1941-1945*, 502-503.
[250] Kamikaze: Suicide bombers
[251] Antony Beevor, *The Second World War* (New York: Little, Brown and Company, 2012), 692

American General Robert L. Eichelberger cooperating with Filipino guerrillas, whose contributions assisted the American efforts to liberate the Philippines.[252]

Battle of Mindoro

As American troops fought in Leyte, American forces began attacking Mindoro, a large island south of Luzon. Strategically, the island would be necessary to build airfields in order to establish American air dominance. Fortunately, the island of Mindoro was only held lightly by the Japanese, while the majority of the island was occupied by Filipino guerillas. Despite Japanese kamikaze attacks on the convoy traveling from Leyte to Mindoro, by December 16th, 1944, the island was secured.[253]

---

[252] U.S. Army, "Special Operations in the Pacific", *U.S. Army Center of Military History,* http://www.history.army.mil/books/wwii/70-42/70-424.html

[253] Dale Andrade, "Luzon" *U.S. Army Center of Military History,* Last Modified October 3 2003, Last Accessed August 4 2017, http://www.history.army.mil/brochures/luzon/72-28.htm.

Battle of Luzon and the Raid of Cabanatuan

On January 9th of 1945, the first American units landed on Luzon, followed by the successful recapture of Clark Field air base.[254] The advance towards Manila continued from both the north and south, effectively securing the Bataan Peninsula. On January 9th of 1945, [255] a large naval bombardment and landing on the Lingayen Gulf, signalled the arrival of Allied troops prepared to recapture Luzon. As the troops began their drive down to Manila, MacArthur ordered prison raids to free American and Filipino POWs and internees.

On January 30th, 1945, Filipino guerrillas, the rangers of the 6th Ranger Battalion, and the Alamo Scouts, rescued over 500 Allied prisoners from the Cabanatuan Prison Camp. The liberating forces needed to act quickly in fear of a repeated incident of the Palawan Massacre, where Allied prisoners of war were burned to death by Japanese who feared American forces were coming.[256] In the daring raid of Cabanatuan, about 280 Filipino guerrillas under the leadership of Capt. Eduardo Joson and Capt. Juan Pajota, guided the American forces through 20 miles of enemy territory. The Filipino guerrillas were stationed around the prison camp, creating roadblocks to hold off enemy troops from coming from Cabanatuan City. The liberating force was small compared to the possibility of 7,000-8,000 Japanese troops who could have counter attacked. In this heroic rescue attempt, only two American soldiers died and 21 Filipino guerrillas were

---

[254] "Luzon" *U.S. Army Center of Military History.*
[255] Patrick K. O'Donnell, *Into the Rising Sun* (New York: The Free Press, 2002), 175.
[256] See page 25-26.

wounded, while the Japanese suffered greater casualties. [257] Camp O'Donnell was also liberated on January 30th. [258]

American divisions continued to land at Bataan to drive Japanese out of Manila using both aerial and artillery attacks. By February, troops surrounded Manila, in position to invade.

Corregidor and the Raid of Los Banos

On Feb 16th, US troops attacked Corregidor, which was necessary to block Manila Bay. Enemy resistance on Corregidor ended by February 27th of 1945.[259] Although MacArthur underestimated the number of Japanese forces on Corregidor, both infantrymen and paratroopers were able to hold off Japanese defense until the resistance ended on March 2nd, 1945.[260]

Again fearing the Japanese would massacre the inmates, MacArthur planned a raid on the civilian internment camp of Los Banos even before the Battle of Corregidor ended.[261] With the help of Filipino guerrillas, the American forces planned a land, water, and air attack while the guards were most vulnerable. American division Scouts and Filipino guerrillas surrounded the camp at night. When the U.S. Parachute B company dropped down to land the next morning on February 23rd, 1945, the American and Filipino forces began their assault on the Japanese. The Americans fired guns while the Filipinos attacked the Japanese with machet-

---

[257] History Channel. *Shootout: Raid on Bataan Death Camp.* Directed by Louis C. Tarantino, 2006. https://www.youtube.com/watch?v=YY9V7vPK5-8
[258] Gordon L. Rottman, *The Cabanatuan Prison Raid: The Philippines 1945* (Osprey Publishing, 2009),7.
[259] O'Donnell, *Into the Rising Sun,* 195.
[260] O'Donnell, *Into the Rising Sun,* 194-5.
[261] O'Donnell, *Into the Rising Sun,* 195.

es. The joint force was successful in rescuing all 2,147 civilian internees from the camp.[262]

Battle of Manila and the Massacre of Manila

35,000 American troops led by Maj. Gen. Joseph Swing and 3,000 Hunter ROTC Filipino guerillas led by Lt. Col. Emmanuel V. de Ocampo fought the month long battle of Manila from February 3rd to March 3rd of 1945.[263] Ignoring Yamashita's orders to evacuate, Rear Admiral Sanji Iwabuchi decided to fight "to the last man", and bloody destruction ensued. American and Filipino troops fought a street war, using the city of Manila as a battleground where many civilians were caught in the crossfire. Filipino civilians would risk their lives to show their gratitude, handing out cigars and candies to fighting American soldiers.[264]

Faced with the fierce attacks by American and Filipino forces, the Japanese took out their anger on innocent civilians. During the massacre of Manila, an estimated 100,000 civilians were killed by bombardment, as well as indiscriminately raped and murdered. War crimes included: the beheading, bayoneting, and shooting of unarmed civilians, including men, women, and children; setting fire to buildings holding large numbers of civilians; torturing of civilians and prisoners of war for information; forcing young girls and women to become comfort women; and the murder of refugees, doctors, and nurses at the Philippines Red Cross. Filipinos were rounded up at various locations throughout Manila, such as Fort Santiago, La Concordia College, and the St. Paul College Chapel, to be killed by the Japanese.[265]

---

[262] History Channel, *Rescue at Dawn: The Los Banos raid*, 2004. https://www.youtube.com/watch?v=ppH0JLaThEE
[263] History Channel, *Rescue at Dawn: The Los Banos raid*.
[264] The Big Picture, United States Army, *Battle of Manila*, 1950-63. https://www.youtube.com/watch?v=j3l6d_o1mxc&t=439s
[265] GOVPH, "BRIEFER: Massacres in the Battle of Manila," *Philippine Presiden-*

A soldier surveys the remains of the Filipinos who were brutally murdered by Japanese troops in Manila. [266]

American forces were able to liberate the Bilibid prison, where POWs were held after the battle of Corregidor. On February 3rd, 1945, the Santo Tomas Camp where approximately 32,000 Americans, 1,000 citizens of Allied countries, and around 100 Filipinos, were held during the Japanese occupation, was also liberated.[267] The internees were largely American families.

[268] Nearing the end of the battle, the remaining Japanese resistance were cornered into the Intramuros, the city within the walls, a Spanish historic site. Without an escape and without even the inkling of an idea of surrender, American

---

tial *Museum & Library*, Last Accessed July 30th, 2017, http://malacanang.gov.ph/75083-briefer-massacres-in-the-battle-of-manila/

[266] U.S. Army, "Special Operations in the Pacific", *U.S. Army Center of Military History.*
[267] Burgess, "Santo Tomas Camp."
[268] The Big Picture, United States Army, *Battle of Manila.*

forces continued to intensely assault the Intramuros. Filipinos would assist by pointing out the Japanese firing positions. After crossing the Pasig river separating the opposing forces, the American troops were finally able to penetrate the walls of the Intramuros and reconquer the rest of Manila. Upon arriving into the Intramuros, the soldiers found the many dead bodies of Filipino civilians caught in the crossfire. The few survivors were evacuated for medical attention.[269]

Prisoners liberated from the Santo Tomas Internment camp, the Japanese ignored many basic necessities of the prisoners, who would physically suffer from lack of food and medicine supplies. [270]

---

[269] The Big Picture, United States Army, *Battle of Manila*.
[270] U.S. Army Signal Corps, "Emaciated Internees at Santo Tomas Internment Camp," February 1945.http://www.west-point.org/family/japanese-pow/POW%20Photos.htm

Filipino citizens of Manila flee from burning buildings in the suburbs.[271]

Although the battle of Manila was declared an American victory, three fourths of Manila was devastated including Intramuros, which held historical significance. The casualties amounted to 25,000 American soldier deaths and an astonishing 125,000 Filipino inhabitant deaths.[272]

---

[271] Robert Ross Smith, *Triumph in the Philippines*, (Washington D.C.,1991)
[272] Costello, *The Pacific War: 1941-1945*, 534.

American soldiers walk among the rubble of Intramuros, which was destroyed during the Battle of Manila.[273]

---

[273] Robert Ross Smith, *Triumph in the Philippines,* (Washington D.C.,1991)

An overview of the city of Manila following the immensely destructive battle of Manila.[274]

Southern Philippines and the Liberation of Mindanao:

While fighting continued in Manila,[275] American troops and Filipino guerrillas began the liberation of the Southern Philippines. The efforts of the guerrillas greatly contributed to the American successes. When MacArthur ordered the start of operations in the Southern Philippines on February 6th, 1945, many of his troops discovered that their work had already been completed by Filipino guerrillas.[276]

On March 10th, 1945, a large guerrilla force helped an American engineer to create a landing strip on Mindanao. Although progress was slowed by a Japanese attack, cooperation between the American infantry, guerrillas, and the Marines forced the Japanese to retreat.[277]

---

[274] Robert Ross Smith, *Triumph in the Philippines*, 301.
[275] Beevor, *The Second World War*, 695.
[276] Beevor, *The Second World War*, 695.
[277] Supreme Commander of the Allied Powers, General Staff of General MacArthur, *Reports of General MacArthur: The Campaigns of MacArthur in the Pacific, Vol. I.* (Library of Congress, 1966), 355.

Filipino guerrillas fighting alongside the American 1st Cavalry Division.[278]

End of Campaign & Aftermath

General MacArthur continued to plan on liberating Philippines island by island. Fighting continued until the official surrender of General Yamashita on September 2nd, 1945, about a month after the atomic bombs on Nagasaki and Hiroshima. By then, the half a million Japanese troops were now forced into various pockets of resistance. [279]

Following the end of World War II, the many atrocities committed in the Philippines towards Filipino and American soldiers and civilians were brought closer to justice during the Tokyo Trials and other military tribunals.

General Massaharu Homma was convicted of war crimes

---

[278] U.S. Army Center of Military History, "Special Operations in the Pacific", page 89.

[279] Supreme Commander of the Allied Powers, General Staff of General MacArthur, *Reports of General MacArthur: The Campaigns of MacArthur in the Pacific, Vol. I.* (Library of Congress, 1966), 465.

including: the Death March of Bataan, the atrocities that occurred in the POW camps at Camp O'Donnell and Cabanatuan, executed by firing squad on April 3rd, 1946.

General Seiichi Terada was accused of not preventing the Palawan Massacre at the Puerto Princesa camp, sentenced to life in Tokyo Prison.[280]

General Tomoyuki Yamashita convicted of the Manila massacre and other related atrocities in a publicized trial in Manila, found guilty and executed by hanging on February 23rd, 1946.

There was no charge or conviction for the sexual slavery Filipina comfort women had to endure. To this day, there has been no formal apology[281].

The Japanese War Crime trial of General Masaharu Homma in Manila.[282]

---

[280] Bob Wilkbanks, *Last Man Out: Glenn McDole, USMC, Survivor of the Palawan Massacre in World War II*, (Jefferson: McFarland, 2004), 144.
[281] Whaley, "In Philippines, World War II's Lesser Known Sex Slaves Speak Out."
[282] "Japanese War Crime trials, Manila," *Department of Defense, National Ar-*

chives, Last Modified, September 18, 1947, Last Accessed August 1, 2017. https://catalog.archives.gov/id/292610

CHAPTER 7
The Legacy of the Philippines and Its Peoples' Roles in World War II

A 1950 war film directed by Fritz Lang that depicts the Anglo American perspective of guerrilla warfare in the Philippines.[283]

---

[283] Movie Poster Shop,"Americann Guerrilla in the Philippines, 1950," *Movie Poster Shop*, Last Accessed August 1st, 2017, http://www.moviepostershop.com.

Many depictions of the liberation of the Philippines would be memorialized in Hollywood films, plays, and music. The 1945 Hollywood propaganda film, *Back to Bataan,* starring John Wayne would be one of the first depictions of the Pacific Theater that demonstrated to American audiences the roles of Filipino guerrillas throughout the Japanese occupation of the Pacific.[284] Other films like the 1950 American war film, *An American Guerrilla in the Philippines*, starred an all star cast with major director, Fritz Lang. Despite the historical background and environment of the film, none of the leading cast members were Filipino.[285] Lang's post war film depicts that the guerrillas responsible for creating and opening networks of communication for the Allied forces and underground resistance were solely the efforts of American resistance fighters, not Filipinos. Although the film was not very successful at the box office, its themes of American guerrilla contributions would define the guerrilla resistance in the Philippines as purely American led. Films and war narratives popularized during the Post War Era would continue to upstage and conceal the roles of Filipina/o guerrillas throughout the latter half of the twentieth century while the geo-political state of the newly sovereign Philippines would attempt to rebuild and consolidate its new democratic government, societies, and natural landscape leveled during the war.

The entrance into the Cold War and the Philippines newly achieved Independence led to a continued relationship with the United States. The Philippines economy increased and was a major hub of the Pacific as their ties with the United States continued to improve throughout the Cold War. With

---

com/american-guerrilla-in-the-philippines-movie-poster-1950.

[284] *Back to Bataan*, Directed by Edward Dmytryk, featuring John Wayne, Anthony Quinn, RKO Radio Pictures, 1945.

[285] *An American Guerrilla in the Philippines*, Directed by Fritz Lang, featuring Tyrone Power, Michele Presl, 20th Century Fox, 1950.

the Philippines serving as a strategic blockade to Communism in the Pacific for American Presidents Truman, Eisenhower, Kennedy, Lyndon B. Johnson, and Nixon, the Philippines would continue to receive monetary means to rebuild its nation's infrastructures.

The Cold War on a global scale, although its history is full of landmarks in the expansion of human rights, civil rights, the end of western imperial holdings, and technological advances, is a time period that is rife with political and social turmoil. The Philippines, despite its struggle to become an independent and model Asian developed state, also experienced discontent and disagreement among its Filipino citizenry and Pacific neighbors. These quarrels over political, religious, ethnic, and social ideologies ironically stemmed from the efforts of the diverse guerrilla forces that helped liberate the Philippines from tyranny and bureaucratic chaos.

Inter-Filipino Political, Religious, Ethnic, and Cultural Tensions and Their Effects on the Legacies of the Underground Resistance

The Huks' Entry into the Cold War

Taruc's political platform would affect the way in which the Huks would be treated after the war. MacArthur would continue to have his agents monitor Taruc's Huks throughout Luzon long after the conclusion of the war. The socialist agenda and the group's previous history of seeking to head a communist Philippines independent of American influences would further cement divisions felt between political parties and between socioeconomic classes. Into the post-war era, competition between political ideologies would grow. Democratic states and those arguing for socialist platforms divided the geopolitical landscape in every region of the world attempting to rebuild their governments and economies in the aftermath of World War II. Taruc along with other prominent Communist leaders would attain seats in the newly formed Philippine House of Representatives arguing for social and economic reforms. Due to their conflicting political ideologies, however, the Huks were perceived as a threat to the new democratic establishment. Along with those political biases, the assassinations and raids conducted by radical Huk veterans throughout central Luzon painted the Huk leader Taruc in a negative light. Taruc was removed from his seat in Congress and forced to flee and disband whatever was left of his Huk units even further despite the previous Huk disbandment MacArthur ordered (MacArthur ordered the surrender and disbandment of Taruc's original guerrilla squadrons in 1945 after the liberation of the Philippines from the Japanese occupation).[286]

Taruc's Huks would in turn change their name to the People's Liberation Army (Hukbong Magpagpalaya ng Bayan) in 1950 and would continue guerrilla warfare tactics (raids, kidnapping, takeover of small villages and barrios, etc.) in order to gain more ground and influence for their socialist movement in retaliation to the new independent government, the Third Philippine Republic, headed by Manuel A. Roxas, a fellow guerrilla leader and veteran of the Philippine Commonwealth Army under USAFFE.[287]

Taruc and his guerrillas would historically be labeled by MacArthur's general staff and record keepers as bandits, non-cooperative, passive and non responsive liberation fighters, quick to infighting and competing with other guerrilla organizations. Playing off anti-communist rhetoric common to the Cold War period, Taruc and his entire guerrilla organization would be portrayed negatively and depicted as

---

[286] Ronald E. Dolan, ed. *Philippines: A Country Study* (Washington: GPO for the Library of Congress, 1991), 45-47, 246, 280.

[287] Napoleon D. Valeriano & Charles T. Bohannan, *Counter-Guerrilla Operations: The Philippine Experience* (Westport: Praeger Security International, 2006), 103.

rapists, violent raiders, and communist radicals who abused the peasant class rather than helping to represent or liberate them.[288] Although sources differ as to the overall positive image of Taruc and his Huk peers, their influence in Luzon would be quashed when American President Truman implemented America's aggressive foreign policy, the Truman Doctrine.

Truman's policy, enacted in 1950, focused on eliminating strands of communism abroad by supplying the Philippine government. The Philippines, which still tried to maintain friendly relations with the United States after the war were thus provided with supplies and troops to mitigate, if not eliminate, the associated Huk insurrections on Luzon.[289] Under the presidency of Ramon Magsaysay, the Huk movement would continue to be monitored and further disarmed. By 1955, the Huks would represent very little of the military force and political ideologies that they began prior to World War II.[290] The Cold War period would unfortunately continue to cast all Huk veterans as politically radical and violent insurgents, which in turn would influence Huk veterans from properly being recognized as official World War II participants eligible for pensions and benefits from either the Philippine or American governments.

Like many other Filipino guerrilla troops throughout the last sixty years, Huk veterans would pursue an ongoing legal battle for Huk compensation and recognition. Female Huk veteran, Commander Guerrero, also known as Simeona Punsalan, would fight for the recognition and pensions for surviving members of the Huk forces who fought throughout World War II until her death in 2015 at the age of 93.[291]

---

[288] Benedict J. Kerkvliet, *The Huk Rebellion: A Study of Peasant Revolt in the Philippines* (Berkeley: University of California Press, 1977), 247.
[289] Kerkvliet, *The Huk Rebellion*, 192.
[290] Kerkvliet, *The Huk Rebellion*, 254, 263.
[291] Tonette Orejas, "Last Woman Huk Leader Dies, Leaves Legacy of Dedica-

By 2014, Punsalan helped over 100 Huk veterans apply for pensions and correct military documents and records, putting her thumbprint and adding her recollections of the Huk guerrillas as evidence of the major contributions Huk World War II guerrillas made in the Pacific.

Post World War II International Relations: Philippines, China, and the United States

The Cold War represented a divide and lack of constructive political conversations between the western democratic nations and those of the communist states around the globe. As the Cold War began to quickly take root, and America began to solidify its position as a leader of the "Free World," the Asian regions of the Pacific served as an opportunity to not only block any communist presence or influence, but also as an American opportunity to conduct trade with the Philippines which had valuable natural resources and food products. The Philippines and the United States continued to have friendly international relations after the Philippines gained its independence on July 4th, 1946. The Philippines like many of its neighbors had been ravaged economically and politically by the Japanese imperial presence throughout the war. Through the Bell Act, the United States provided monetary benefits ($800 million) to help the Philippines invigorate its economy while the United States benefitted from equal opportunity to own and build industries that manufactured and extracted goods from the Philippines.[292] This act allowed American entrepreneurs the same opportunities and rights to natural resources and legal influence over private

---

tion," *The Philippine Inquirer, Central Luzon*, July 3rd, 2015, Last Accessed July 16th, 2017, http://newsinfo.inquirer.net/702422/last-woman-huk-leader-dies-leaves-legacy-of-dedication.

[292] Yves Boquet, *The Philippine Archipelago* (Dijon: Springer, 2017), 101.

industry as a Filipino citizen thus disregarding the liberties and priorities of naturalized Philippine citizenry.[293]

The early half of the Cold War Era of the Philippines represented a high time for Filipino trade, a booming economy, reconstruction of a newly independent Philippines ushered in an "amiable" economic and diplomatic relationship with the United States. The Philippines signed not only the Bell Act in 1946, but would also sign a military assistance agreement in 1947 that allowed for a 99 year lease on naval, military, and air bases for the American military.[294]

Clark Air Base and Subic Bay would become the main major military hubs and outlets for the American military and government to pursue their anti-communist policy in Southeast Asia while maintaining their military and political presence in the Philippines. It wasn't until the end of the Cold War in 1992 that the Philippine senate voted not to renew America's 1947 lease agreement to remain in operation at Subic Bay.[295] Despite this eviction of the American military presence for over twenty five years, the alliance and "paternalistic" relationship stemming from the Spanish American War, the Philippine-American War, and World War II has allowed for the Philippines to receive foreign aid from the United States since its independence in 1946.[296] Although foreign aid provided by the United States benefits the Philippines with over $200 million as of 2016 to restructure and build both their economy and military, the legacy of imperi-

---

[293] Boquet, *The Philippine Archipelago*, 101.
[294] Jon Sterngass, The New Immigrants: *Filipino Americans* (New York: Chelsea House Publishers, 2007), 32.
[295] Philip Shenon, "Aquino Revokes Eviction Notice for a U.S. Base," *New York Times*, Last Modified September 18th, 1991, Last Accessed July 28th, 2017, http://www.nytimes.com/1991/09/18/world/aquino-revokes-eviction-notice-for-a-us-base.html.
[296] Frontera, "How Much Foreign Aid Does the Philippines Receive From the United States?" *Frontera News*, Last Modified October 2nd, 2016, Last Accessed July 28th, 2017, https://fronteranews.com/news/asia/much-foreign-aid-manila-lose-washington/.

alism and the economic dependency of colonial territories in the West remains.[297]

Foreign Relations Between the Philippines & China

China and the Philippines' relationship in the last ten years has been strained due to maritime boundary disputes in the Pacific over the control of natural resources in the South Pacific. Both the Chinese and Philippine navy have confronted one another often reaching a standoff over the territorial dispute of the South China Sea and West Philippine Sea borders. Within that region, particularly the Panatag Shoal, designated officially as Philippine Maritime jurisdiction by the Hague-based International Arbitration Tribunal in 2015, the Chinese government has continued to maintain a military presence in the disputed shoals attempting to create military, industry, and government centers in the contested area.[298] Their presence has affected Filipino fishermen in their means of subsistence and income, leading the current president Duterte to attempt diplomatic cooperation over ownership and use of the shoals with the Chinese rather than referring to a confrontational end to Philippine-Chinese relations.[299] The maritime dispute drove the Philippines' previous president, Benigno "Noynoy" Aquino III to go so far as to place a hold on the Philippines' participation in the Chinese led

---

[297] Frontera, "How Much Foreign Aid Does the Philippines Receive From the United States?" https://fronteranews.com/news/asia/much-foreign-aid-manila-lose-washington/.

[298] Bob Shead (ASEAN BRIEFING), "The Philippines' Economic and Political Relations with China," *ASEAN BRIEFING: Business Intelligence from Dezan Shera and Associates*, Last Modified April 10th, 2017, Last Accessed July 25th, 2017, http://www.aseanbriefing.com/news/2017/04/10/philippines-economic-political-relations-china.html.

[299] Rommel C. Banlaoi, "Arbitration Ruling and Philippines-China Relations under the Duterte Administration," *The Huffpost, The World Post*, Last Accessed August 1st, 2017, http://www.huffingtonpost.com/rommel-c-banlaoi/philippines-china-duterte_b_10929512.html.

banking institution, the Asian Infrastructure Investment Bank.[300]

The maritime dispute has led the Philippine government and its peoples to protest against, debate, and question their perspectives and foreign policies concerning China. The territorial dispute also has led to the reopening of Subic Bay to allow for the Philippine airforce and navy to revamp its military forces in order to thwart off Chinese encroachment.[301] The reopening of Subic Bay represents an increase in another form of truculent state expansionism of the Chinese. The opportunity in minimizing the encroachment of Chinese industry and presence along the contested shoals, and the increase in military spending and presence in the Philippines taken together form a bleak future in terms of friendly Philippine and Chinese foreign relations.

The current territorial dispute bordering the South China Sea and West Philippine Sea has soured relations between the Philippines and China which has further added to the neglect and political oversight of the collaborative efforts of the Chinese guerrillas and their Filipino peers during World War II. Despite present racial and political tensions, local communities that were directly affected by the Wa Chi and the Ampaw continue to pay homage to the Filipino-Chinese coalition that helped liberate Luzon from the Japanese Occupation. Public monuments (markers and panels) such as the Chinese-Filipino Martyr Memorial Marker located in Manila in front of the historical Binondo Church (also known

---

[300] Bob Shead (ASEAN BRIEFING), "The Philippines' Economic and Political Relations with China," *ASEAN BRIEFING: Business Intelligence from Dezan Shera and Associates*, Last Modified April 10th,2017, Last Accessed July 25th, 2017, http://www.aseanbriefing.com/news/2017/04/10/philippines-economic-political-relations-china.html.

[301] The Guardian Philippines Staff, "Philippines Reopens Subic Bay as Military Base to Cover South China Sea," *The Guardian, Philippines*, Last Modified July 15th, 2015, Last Accessed July 30th, 2017, https://www.theguardian.com/world/2015/jul/16/philippines-reopens-subic-bay-as-military-base-to-cover-south-china-sea.

as the Holy Rosary Parish Church), continue to honor the legacy of warmer and more successful Philippine and Chinese coalitions. Many of the Chinese-Filipino Guerrilla Martyr monuments can be found throughout Manila's historical Chinatown district.

In the municipality of Candaba in the province of Pampanga of Central Luzon, the local communities still pay homage to the Wa Chi guerrillas who safeguarded their homes and well being throughout the war. The Wa Chi 48th squadron veterans also have continued to work towards paying back the communities of Candaba who helped hide their underground resistance and housed them when they were low on resources during the war.[302] The surviving Wa Chi veterans and their families through programs like the "Operation Barrio Schools Project" in partnership with the Federation of Chinese-Filipino Chamber of Commerce and Industry have pulled together to erect various school buildings throughout the municipality of Candaba and the province of Laguna.[303]

The markers and panels originally displayed to the public in the summer of 1995 on behalf of the Confederation of Filipino-Chinese Veterans, along with community programs like "Operation Barrio Schools Project" together continue to have symbolic purpose in regards to Philippine-Chinese foreign affairs. Both continue to serve as small daily reminders of the historic collaborative efforts of Filipinos and Chinese citizens who once shared a common goal of salvaging Asian communities and their cultural impact in the Pacific.

Short Lived Peace In Mindanao

Similar to the strained territorial relations between the

---

[302] Mundo, "Wa Chi's 48th Squadron's 70th Anniversary: Heroism and Friendship."
[303] Mundo, "Wa Chi's 48th Squadron's 70th Anniversary: Heroism and Friendship."

Chinese government and the Philippines, the Moros of the southern islands of the Philippines have also bumped heads with Philippine presidents within the last seventy years over their ancestral lands and right to become a sovereign Muslim state. Both groups of these age old disputes, Filipino Christians and Moros, are responsible for violent excursions against the other party within the last twenty years thus contributing and perpetuating centuries worth of religious and cultural hostilities.

After the liberation of the Philippines in World War II, decades of violence would ensue and be initiated by both the Christian Filipinos and the Moros further adding to the previous colonial era's cultural and religious rivalries. In the aftermath of the terrorist attack of the trade centers in New York on September 11th, 2001, American and international media coverage, and anti-terrorist military and government initiatives targeted at Muslim terrorist groups around the globe increased. Islamic extremists like the Abu Sayyaf have also gathered more followers to their independence movement in Mindanao and the southern islands of the Philippines.

The Abu Sayyaf and a more recent radical group ISIL (Islamic State of Iraq and the Levant) have staged various hostile demonstrations to highlight their desire to break from the Philippines' Republic (i.e. bombing, murdering, kidnapping, extortion, and public executions) as ways to argue and forcibly have acknowledged their political goals for an independent Muslim state in the Philippines.[304] One of their main goals that bolsters their radical rhetoric is their discontent as to the legacy of western imperialism in the Philippines, as seen with America's military and economic interventions in Asia.

With the presence of numerous terrorist organizations on

---

[304] Spencer C. Tucker, ed., *Encyclopedia of Insurgency and Counterinsurgency: A New Era of Modern Warfare* (Santa Barbara: ABC-CLIO, 2013), 367.

Mindanao like the Abu Sayyaf and ISIL, the collaborative endeavors of the Filipino Christians and Moro guerrillas have received little to no recognition outside of Wendell Fertig's memoirs and author John C. Keats' 1963's interpretation of the Pacific Theater on Mindanao, *They Fought Alone*. With the onslaught of terrorist activity, and the increasing cultural and social divide between Filipino Muslims and Christians, the efforts of the unified guerrilla units of Christians and Muslims of World War II will remain as a rare and isolated event of teamwork and compromise. The emergence of ISIL alone has led to collaborations among three radical Islamic groups (Maute "Islamic State of Lanao", Abu Sayyaf, and ISIL) on the southern Philippine islands further amplifying religious and cultural tensions leading to the 2016 terrorist bombing in the city of Davao and more recently, the May 2017 Battle of Marawi.

The ongoing Battle of Marawi, also known as the Marawi Siege, involved the Philippine government taking an offensive stance to remove Islamic terrorist leaders out of Marawi, a city in the province of Lanao del Sur. The offensive strategy resulted in the Maute/ISIL takeover of the city pushing both Christian and Muslim civilians to evacuate and escape the brutalities of the extremists who continue to be in pursuit of pushing out Filipino Christians and removing Philippine government jurisdiction out of the region.[305] The casualties and hostilities from these recent terrorist activities have forced President Rodrigo Duterte to enact martial law on the island of Mindanao till December 2017.[306] With such political strife taking hold of Mindanao, the efforts of Fertig's

---

[305] Yasmeen Serhan, "The ISIS-Linked Takeover of a Philippines City," *The Atlantic*, Last Modified May 30th, 2017, Last Accessed August 4th, 2017, https://www.theatlantic.com/news/archive/2017/05/philippines-isis/528531/.

[306] Felipe Villamor, "Philippines Congress Extends Martial Law in Besieged Region," *The New York Times*, Last Modified July 22nd, 2017, Last Accessed July 30th, 2017, https://www.nytimes.com/2017/07/22/world/asia/philippines-martial-law-rodrigo-duterte.html.

guerrillas have failed to be recognized by their descendents as a historical lesson of the possibilities of a peaceful, cooperative, and united Filipino and Moro cultural presence and community on Mindanao.

The Continuing Battles for the Philippine Guerrillas Seventy Five Years Later

After the official liberation of the Philippines in September of 1945, American President Harry Truman rescinded all moral and monetary compensation to the Filipino/a guerrilla fighters. The Rescission Act of 1946 denied Filipino/a veterans any benefits promised to them (immigration privileges to the United States, or full American military benefits including healthcare, educational scholarships, and official recognition by the American government).[307] Not all Filipino soldiers were denied these benefits, particularly a number of Filipino soldiers who served in the USAFFE. But for the majority of guerrillas who fought alongside the American USAFFE soldiers, rebuilding the Philippines and their communities with little to no aid from the American leaders who requested and benefited from the Filipino guerrillas' sacrifices, recognition would require excessive paperwork and major changes to the typical historical narrative of the liberation of the Philippines. The post war and Cold War eras would prove to be another physical and psychological struggle for hundreds of thousands of Filipino/a veterans.

Both Franklin Delano Roosevelt and Truman's administration's refusal to follow through on their promise of allow-

---

[307] Emil Guillermo, "Forgotten: The Battle Thousands of World War II Veterans Are Still Fighting," *NBC News Asian America*, Last Modified February 18th, 2016, Last Accessed July 27th, 2017, http://www.nbcnews.com/news/asian-america/forgotten-battle-thousands-wwii-veterans-are-still-fighting-n520456.

ing both Filipino and Filipino American World War II veterans military benefits would prove to be a lasting detriment and dishonor to the past and living memory of the Philippine Resistance. It was not until recently under the Obama Administration that surviving Filipino/a guerrillas residing in the United States were issued recognition for their service. Under the Filipino Veteran's Equity Compensation Act of 2009, Filipino veterans of World War II living in the United States would receive a lump sum of $15,000 for their services. For those surviving veterans who continue to reside in the Philippines, they would receive a lump sum of $9,000.[308] Despite the good intentions of the monetary compensation, the legal road for veterans to attain the lump sum continues to be difficult.

Many veterans and their families in both the Philippines and the United States have experienced denials to their applications for various reasons. Filipino guerrillas used pseudonyms to avoid capture by Japanese spies and thus labeled their service name as different from their given names.[309] Other guerrillas and veterans like the Aetas of Luzon, whom many were illiterate, find the paperwork process just as difficult to complete and justify due to the expenses required for indigenous peoples to leave their ancestral homes and take on lawyers to help prove their veteran status.[310] For Filipinos and Filipino Americans residing in the United States, attempts at finding the proper military records to prove one's veteran status is also rather expensive and requires the aid

---

[308] Emil Guillermo, "Thousands of Filipino-American World War II Vets Make Appeals Over Equity Pay Denial," *NBC News Asian America*, Last Modified November 11th, 2015, Last Accessed July 28th, 2017, http://www.nbcnews.com/news/asian-america/thousands-filipino-american-wwii-vets-make-appeals-over-equity-pay-n460151.

[309] Guillermo, "Thousands of Filipino-American World War II Vets Make Appeals Over Equity Pay Denial."

[310] Tonnette Orejas, "Pension Elusive for Aeta Guerrillas."

of hired researchers who can navigate the archives known as the Philippine Archive Collection located at the National Archives and Record Administration maintained in College Park, Maryland. The monetary and physical process of travelling, navigating legal records, and having the legal know how to fill out the the appropriate applications are taxing hurdles for many of the surviving senior citizens. The applications for both Veteran status and the Filipino Veterans Equity Compensation Fund, via the Department of Veterans Affairs, has proven to be no easy feat for senior citizens, let alone their families.

Although some veterans have received their veterans benefits (these include healthcare and naturalization) from the United States government, many of those same veterans were refused the lump sum payout of the Veterans Equity Fund. As of 2017, many veterans, their widows, and their surviving family members who were approved in 2009 for the lump sum continue to wait for their payout compensation leaving only 18,976 Filipino veterans of the over 250,000 veterans in total to be officially approved and compensated.[311] Nearly 24,000 applications have been denied as of June 2017.[312]

The Philippine veterans and their fight for recognition and acknowledgement for their World War II services share a similar history to the late 1980s monetary and political recognition of the struggles of another ethnically marginalized group; the Japanese Americans. The Japanese-American 442nd Infantry and Japanese American internment camp survivors of World War II would protest and wait nearly

---

[311] Guillermo, "Thousands of Filipino-American World War II Vets Make Appeals Over Equity Pay Denial," http://www.nbcnews.com/news/asian-america/thousands-filipino-american-wwii-vets-make-appeals-over-equity-pay-n460151.

[312] Center for Minority Veterans, "WWII Filipino Veterans Equity Compensation Fund," *US Department of Veterans Affairs*, Last Modified June 1st, 2017, Last Accessed July 29th, 2017, https://www.va.gov/centerforminorityveterans/fvec.asp.

half a century for the U.S. government to address its racially charged actions of Executive Order 9066 (FDR's forcible removal of Japanese and Japanese American citizens into internment camps during World War II).[313] Similar to the 1988 Civil Liberties Act signed by President Ronald Reagan, the Veterans Equity Fund Act serves as a stepping stone for recognizing the legacy of racial prejudices that have allowed for the lack of mention to both the heroes and victims of color of World War II. These same racial and gendered prejudices have led to the lack of discussion as to the ethnic and gendered makeup and diversity of the Allied war efforts that continue to go unheeded and unattended to.

---

[313] Bilal Qureshi, "From Right to Wrong: A U.S. Apology for Japanese Internment," *National Public Radio*, Last Modified August 9th, 2013, Last Accessed August 4th, 2017, http://www.npr.org/sections/codeswitch/2013/08/09/210138278/japanese-internment-redress.

EPILOGUE

Over 250,000 Filipino and Filipino Americans served in World War II. Whether these men and women were guerrillas, USAFFE soldiers, civilian combatants, scouts, guides, nurses, doctors or regular villagers aiding the resistance movement, many of these veterans of war continue to receive little to no government compensation or official recognition in both the Philippines and the United States. Recent documentaries like "Unsurrendered 2" written and directed by Ban Lograno, produced by Lucky Guillermo, pay homage to the memories of the lesser known Filipino and Chinese guerrilla fighters. Social media hub, Facebook, also has served as a haven for World War II veterans to post their experiences on Facebook groups and pages (i.e. The Philippine Diary Project, Philippines Veterans Affairs Office Page, the Valor Project). Social media platforms combined with the work of traditional scholars, veterans, their families, and filmmakers, have helped tremendously in calling attention to the lesser known contributions, and humble heroism, of the various specific guerrilla units that spanned the Philippine Islands.

The majority of public, general audience resources on World War II continue to emphasize and highlight the leadership of General MacArthur whilst sidestepping the roles of the many Filipinos, Filipinas, and ethnic minorities that helped to liberate the Philippines. American History Textbooks like *The American Vision: Modern Times* (whose contributing author includes renowned historian James M. McPherson) mention very little of the Pacific Front. Textbooks like *The American Vision*, silence the Filipino American and Filipino contributions in World War II by only highlighting, again, MacArthur's role in the Pacific. *A History of Western Society: Since 1300* by scholars John P. McKay, Bennett D. Hill, and John Buckler, are also guilty of falling into the same historical narrative of World War II in the Pacific. Another textbook, *The American Pageant*, by history and American Studies scholars (David M. Kennedy, Lizabeth Cohen, and thomas A. Bailey), does offer sections of information that pay tribute to the contributions of Filipino and Filipino Americans within the last century to both America's ethnic and cultural diversity. Nonetheless, the textbook leaves out any details hinting as to how the Allies benefited from the efforts of the Philippines' guerrillas in winning the Pacific Theater.

Perhaps one of the largest landmarks in readdressing historical narratives of the Liberation of the Philippines is American President Barack Obama's approval of the Filipino Veterans of World War II Congressional Gold Medal Act. The Act was initially proposed in 2015 by Hawaiian senator Mazie Hirono, house representative of Hawaii Tulsi Gabbard, and co sponsored by other senators and representatives from California and Nevada. The act formally recognized over 250,000 men and women who responded to President Franklin Delano Roosevelt's "call to duty" and fought under the American flag towards the liberation of the Philippines.[314] Guerrillas also fall under the category of veterans mean-

---

[314] Stephen Bai & Charles Lam, "House Passes Bill to Award Congressional Medal to Filipino World War II Vets," *NBC News Asian America*, Last Modified November 13th, 2016, Last Accessed August 1st, 2017, http://www.nbcnews.com/news/asian-america/house-vote-congressional-gold-medal-filipino-world-war-ii-vets-n689231.

ing that finally women could be recognized as combatants, soldiers, or guerrillas (like Mrs. Lourdes Poblete) therefore making ethnic women visible as vital and active components to World War II.

Other Filipino achievements include a Filipino American History Month which is celebrated in October and recognizes the various roles Filipinos and Filipino Americans have taken in preserving and promoting the basic tenements of American democracy, diversity, and above all, their contributions in World War II. These recent contributions to recognizing the roles of Filipino and Filipino-American historical actors serve as international platforms for the voices of the Filipina/o guerrillas. Thus, the recognition for all those guerrillas and Filipina/o soldiers who sacrificed their lives for freedom and democracy continues to be an uphill battle that only further highlights the Philippine veterans' astounding vigor and fortitude.

One of the bronze monuments that pays homage to the Filipino guerrillas of World War II located at the World War II Memorial on Corregidor.[315]

---

[315] Art Villasanta, "The Filipino Nation-in-Arms and Its Defeat of the Empire of Japan in World War II," *FilipinoNationInArms Blogspot*, Last Modified August 21st, 2013, Last Accessed July 28th, 2017, http://filipinonationinarms.blogspot.com/.

RESOURCES

Stacey Salinas' Resources (Introduction, Chapters 2, 3, 5, 7, Epilogue):

Atwood, Kathryn J. *Women Heroes of World War II: The Pacific Theater, 15 Stories of Resistance, Rescue, Sabotage, and Survival*. Chicago: Chicago Review Press, 2016.

Aviado, Jose D. *The Foundation of Philippine Democracy*. University of California Press-Lexicon, 1960.

Baclagon, Colonel Uldarico S. *The Philippine Resistance Movement Against Japan: 10 December 1941 - 14 June 1945*. Manila: Munoz Press-Veterans Federation of the Philippines, 1966.

Beede, Benjamin R. *The War of 1898, and U.S. Interventions, 1898-1934, an Encyclopedia*. New York: Garland Publishing Inc., 1994.

Bohannan, Charles T. & Napolean D. Valeriano. *Counter-Guerrilla Operations: The Philippine Experience*. Westport:Greenwood Publishing Group ABC-CLIO: 2006.

Brave Host. "Diary of a POW, Herman Beaber." *POW/MIA Ring*. Last Modified March 27th, 2017, Last Accessed July 7th, 2017, http://ithascome.bravehost.com/.

Cogan, Frances B. *Capture: The Japanese Internment of American Civilians in the Philippines, 1941-1945*. Athens: University of Georgia Press, 2000.

Confesor, Tomas. "To Leyte And Washington In 1944–1945 *(A Diary Fragment Of Tomas Confessor).*" *Bulletin of the American Historical Collection*, Vol 10 No. 3 (July 1982).

Constantino, Renato and Letizia R. Constantino. *A History of the Philippines*. New York: Monthly Review Press-New York University Press, 1975.

Leonard Davis. *Revolutionary Struggle in the Philippines*. New York: Palgrave Macmillan Press, 1989.

Deocampo, Nick. *Eiga: Cinema in the Philippines During World War II*. Anvil Publishing, 2016.

Department of Defense. Far East Command. Philippines Command. Guerrilla Affairs Division. HQ

Philippines Command. U.S. Army Recognition Program of Philippine Guerrillas., ca. 1949, National Archives Identifier 6921767, August 1st, 1948 to October 14th, 1949.

De Pedro, Ernie A. "Plaza Dilao in History." *Lord Takayama Jubilee Foundation*. Last Accessed July 6th, 2017. Https://takayamaukon.com/plaza-dilao-in-history/.

Dower, John W. *War Without Mercy: Race & Power in the Pacific War.* New York: Pantheon Books, 1986.

Dowlen, Dorothy Dore & Theresa Kaminski. *Enduring What Cannot Be Endured: Memoir of a Woman Medical Aide in the Philippines in World War II.* Jefferson: McFarland, 2001.

Edwards, Wallace. *Comfort Women: A History of Japanese Forced Prostitution During the Second World War.* Absolute Crime, 2013.

Eisner, Peter. *MacArthur's Spies: The Soldier, the Singer, and the Spymaster who Defied the Japanese in World War II.* New York: Viking-Penguin Random House, 2017.

Felias, Remedios. *The Hidden Battle of Leyte: The Picture Diary of a Girl Taken by the Japanese Military.* Bucung Bucong, 1999.

Franklin, Cynthia G., Ruth Hsu, & Suzanne Kosanke, ed. *Navigating Island and Continents: Conversations and Contestations in and Around the Pacific, Selected Essays, Vol. 17.*

Honolulu: Colleges of Languages, Linguistics and Literature, University of Hawai'i, 2000.

Friend, Theodore. *The Blue-Eyed Enemy: Japan Against the West in Java and Luzon, 1942-1945.* New Jersey: Princeton University Press, 2014.

Fujitani, T., Geoffrey M. White, and Lisa Yoneyama. *Perilous Memories: The Asia-Pacific War(s).* London: Duke University Press, 2001.

Gaerlan, Cecilia. "World War II in the Philippines." *Bataan Legacy Historical Society.* Last Modified July 2017. Last Accessed July 28th, 2017. http://www.bataanlegacy.org/index.html.

Gomez, Hilario Molijan. *The Moro Rebellion and the Search for Peace: A Study on Christian-Muslim Relations in the Philippines.* Silsilah Publications, 2000.

Guardia, Mike. *American Guerrilla: The Forgotten Heroics of Robert W. Volckmann-The Man Who Escaped from Bataan, Raised a Filipino Army Against the Japanese, and Became the True "Father" of the Army Special Forces.* Haverton: Casemate Publishing, 2010.

Hacker, Barton C. & Margaret Vining, ed. *A Companion to Women's Military.* Boston: Brill, 2012.

Heimann, Judith M. *The Airmen and the Headhunters: A True Story of Lost Soldiers, Heroic Tribesmen and the Unlikeliest Rescue of World War II.* Houghton Mifflin Harcourt, 2009.

Henderson, Bruce. *Rescue at Los Banos: The Most Daring Prison Camp Raid of World War II.*

New York: HarperCollins, 2015.

Hogan Jr., David D. *US Army Special Operations in World War II.* Washington D.C.: Center of Military History Department of the Army, 2014.

Holland, Albert E., "The Santo Tomas Internment Camp Diary of Albert E. Holland, 1944-1945" (1945). Trinity College Digital Repository, Hartford, CT.
http://digitalrepository.trincoll.edu/trinarchives/3.

Holmes, Kent. *Wendell Fertig and His Guerrilla Forces in the Philippines: Fighting the Japanese Occupation, 1942-1945.* Jefferson: McFarland & Company, 2015.

Holmes, Virginia Hansen. *Guerrilla Daughter.* Kent University Press, 2009.

Holthe, Tess Uriza. *When the Elephants Dance.* New York: Penguin Books, 2002.

Hunt, Ray C. & Bernard Norling. *Behind Japanese Lines: An American Guerrilla in the Philippines.* University of Press of Kentucky, 2014.

Isip, Manuel Ray. "The Fighting Filipinos: Poster Story." *Filipino Executive Council of Greater Philadelphia.* Last Accessed July 8th, 2017, https://pinoyphilly.com/from-our-editors/the-fighting-filipinos-poster-story/.

Jamboy, Evelyn Mallillin. *The Resistance Movement in Lanao, 1942-1945.* Coordination Center of Research and Development MSU-Iligan Institute of Technology, 2006.

Kaminski, Theresa. *Prisoners in Paradise: American Women in the Wartime South Pacific.* Lawrence: University of Kansas, 2000.

Kaminski, Theresa. *Angels of the Underground: The American Women Who Resisted the Japanese in the Philippines in World War II.* New York: Oxford University Press, 2016.

John Keats. *They Fought Alone: Classics of World War II.* Pennsylvania State University: Time-Life, 2005.

Kerkvliet, Benedict J. *The Huk Rebellion: A Study of Peasant Revolt in the Philippines.*

Berkeley: University of California Press, 1977.

Kintanar, Thelma B., & Clemen C. Aquino, Patricia B. Arinto, Ma. Luisa T. Camagay.

Kuwentong Bayan/Noong Panahoon: Everyday Life in a Time of War (Quezon City: University of the Philippines Press, 2006).

Klein, Ronald D. *The Other Empire: The Literary Views of Japan from the Philippines, Singapore, and Malaysia.* Quezon City: The University of the Philippines Press, 2008.

Kiyosaki, Wayne & Richard Sakakida. *A Spy in their Midst: The World War II Struggle of a Japanese American Hero.* Lanham: Madison Books, 1995.

Kollektor, Pinoy. "Dawn of Freedom - Philippine World War II Japanese Propaganda Film."

Pinoy Kollektor. Last Modified October 12th, 2011. Last Accessed July 8th, 2017. http://pinoykollektor.blogspot.com/2011/10/48-dawn-of-freedom-philippine-wwii.html.

Lamont-Brown, Raymond. *Kempeitai: Japan's Dreaded Military Police*. Sutton, 1998.

Lanzona, Vina A. *Amazons of the Huk Rebellion: Gender, Sex, and Revolution in the Philippines*. Madison: University of Wisconsin Press, 2009.

Lee, Ernesto. *World War II Philippines: A Boy's Tale of Survival*. Xlibris, 2010.

Levine, Alan J. *Captivity, Flight, and Survival in World War II*. Westport: Praeger Greenwood Publishing Group, 2000.

Ling, Huping & Allan W. Austin. *Asian American History and Culture: An Encyclopedia, Volume 1 & 2*. New York: Routledge, 2015.

Luga, Alan R. *Muslim Insurgency in Mindanao, Philippines: A Thesis*, Philippine Military Academy, Baguio City, 1981.

Lukacs, John D. *Escape from Davao: The Forgotten Story of the Most Daring Prison Break of the Pacific War*. New York: New American Library, 2010.

Marking, Yay Panlilio. *The Crucible: An Autobiography by Colonel Yay, Filipina American Guerilla*. New Brunswick: Rutgers University Press, 2009.

Matthiessen, Sven. *Japanese Pan-Asianism and the Philippines from the Late Nineteenth Century to the End of World War II: Going to the Philippines Is like Coming Home?* Brill, 2016.

McCoy, Alfred W., ed., *An Anarchy of Families: State and Family in the Philippines*. Madison: The University of Wisconsin Press, 2009.

McKenna, Thomas M. *Muslim Rulers and Rebels: Everyday Politics and Armed Separatism in the Southern Philippines*. Los Angeles: University of California Press, 1988.

Mojica, Proculo L., *Terry's Hunters: The True Story of the Hunters ROTC Guerrillas*. Benipayo Press, 1965.

Montgomery, Ben. *The Leper Spy: The Story of an Unlikely Hero of World War II*. Chicago: Chicago Review Press, 2017.

Moore, Stephen L., *As Good As Dead: The True Story of Eleven POWs Who Escaped from Palawan Island*. New York: Penguin, 2016.

Moore, William C. Moore. *The Hukbalahap Insurgency, 1948-1954: An Analysis of the Roles, Missions and Doctrine of the Philippine Military Forces*. Army War College Carlisle Barracks, 1971.

Nakano, Satoshi. "The Filipino World War II Veterans Equity Movement and the Filipino American Community." *Hitotsubashi Journal of Social Studies* 32, 2000: 33-53.

Norling, Bernard. *The Intrepid Guerrillas of Northern Luzon*. Lexington: University Press of Kentucky, 2005.

Office of Global Issues. *Insurgency in the Philippines: Organization and Capabilities*.

Washington: Central Intelligence Agency, 1985.

Ohl, John Kennedy. *Minutemen: The Military Career of Robert S. Beightler*. Boulder: Lynne Reinner Publishers, 2001.

Planta, Mercedes G. "*Sakdalistas' Struggle for Philippine Independence,1930-1945*, Review."

Philippine Studies: Historical and Ethnographic Viewpoints Vol. 63, No. 4 (December 2014): 589-593.

Ramsey, Edwin Price & Stephen J. Rivele. *Lieutenant Ramsey's War: From Horse Soldier to Guerrilla Commander*. Brassey's, 1990.

Real Sons and Daughters of Ifugao. "Battle of Kiangan: The Pacific Battle of World War II

Ended Here." *RSDI Freedom Wall*. Last Modified February 8th, 2016. Last Accessed

July 8th, 2017. http://www.armchairgeneral.com/trek-to-kiangan-and-back.htm.

Romulo, Carlos P. *I Saw the Fall of the Philippines*. New York: Doubleday, 1944.

Romulo, Carlos P. *I See the Philippines Rise*. New York: Doubleday, 1946.

Rudi, Norman. *Lang: The World War II Story of an American Guerrilla on Mindanao, Philippine Islands*. Madison: McMillen Publishing, 2003.

Ryan, Allyn C. *RM: A Biographical Novel of Ramon Magsaysay*. Xlibris Corporation, 2007.

Schirmer, Daniel B., Stephen Rosskamm Shalom. *The Philippines Reader: A History of Colonialism,Neocolonialism, Dictatorship, and Resistance*. Cambridge: South End Press, 1987.

Schmidt, Larry S. *American Involvement in the Filipino Resistance Movement on Mindanao During the Japanese Occupation, 1941-1945*. Fort Leavenworth: United States Marine Corps, 1982.

Sides, Hampton. *Ghost Soldiers:The Forgotten Epic Story of World War II's Most Dramatic Mission*. New York: Random House, 2001.

Smith, Robert Ross & the Defense Dept., Army, Center of Military History. *US Army in World War II, War in the Pacific, Triumph in the Philippines*. Washington D.C.: Center of Military History - United States Army, 1993.

Silbey, David. *A War of Frontier and Empire: The Philippine-American War, 1899-1902*. New York: Macmillan, 2008.

Sinclair II, Major Peter T. *Men of Destiny: The American and Filipino*

Guerrillas During the Japanese Occupation of the Philippines. Pickle Partners Publishing, 2015.

Stanton, Shelby L. Order of Battle: U.S. Army, World War II. Presidio Press, 1984.

Sterngass, Jon. The New Immigrants: Filipino Americans. New York: Chelsea House Publishers, 2007.

Supreme Commander of the Allied Powers, General Staff of General MacArthur. Reports of

General MacArthur: The Campaigns of MacArthur in the Pacific, Vol. I. Library of Congress, 1966.

Syjuco, Felisa A. The Kempei Tai in the Philippines, 1941-1945. Quezon City: New Day Publishers, 1988.

Tan, Andrew H. A Handbook of Terrorism and Insurgency in Southeast Asia. Northampton: Edward Elgar Publishing, 2009.

Taruc, Luis. Born of the People. New York: International Publishers, 1953.

Tucker, Spencer C., ed. Encyclopedia of Insurgency and Counterinsurgency: A New Era of Modern Warfare. Santa Barbara: ABC-CLIO, 2013.

UCA News. "Japanese Priest Who Worked in the Philippines During War Honored."

UCA News: Asia's Most Trusted Catholic News Source. Last Modified March 9th, 1993. Last Accessed July 6th, 2017.

Http://www.ucanews.com/story-archive/?post_name=/1993/03/09/japanese-priest
-who-worked-in-philippines-during-war-honored&post_id=42928.

Valeriano, Napoleon D. & Charles T. Bohannan. Counter-Guerrilla Operations: The Philippine Experience. Westport: Praeger Security International, 2006.

Welch, Bob. Resolve: From the Jungles of WWII BAtaan, the Epic Story of a Soldier, a Flag, and a Promise Kept. New York: Berkley Publishing Group, 2012.

Willoughby, Charles Andrew. The Guerrilla Resistance Movement in the Philippines: 1941-1945. New York: Vantage Press, 1972.

World War II Foundation. "Film Details Local War Hero's Exploits." World War II Foundation.

Last Modified 2017, Last Accessed July 7th, 2017.

http://www.wwiifoundation.org/2015/09/13/film-details-local-war-heros-exploits/.

Klytie Xu's Resources (Chapters 1, 4, 6):

Anderson, Charles R. "Leyte." U.S. Army Center of Military History. Last Modified October 3 2003. Last Accessed August 3, 2017. http://www.history.army.mil/brochures/leyte/leyte.htm

Andrade, Dale. "Luzon." *U.S. Army Center of Military History*. Last Modified October 3 2003. Last Accessed August 4 2017. http://www.history.army.mil/brochures/luzon/72-28.htm

The Associated Press. "Wartime Workers in the Philippines to Sue Japanese Companies." *The New York Times*. Last Modified March 27, 2000. Last Accessed July 27, 2017. http://www.nytimes.com/2000/03/27/world/wartime-workers-in-the-philippines-to-sue-japanese-companies.html?mcubz=1

Beevor, Antony. *The Second World War*. New York: Little, Brown and Company, 2012.

Berg, Tom. "Death March survivor finally tells story." *Orange County Register*. Last Modified May 17, 2012. Accessed July 31, 2017. http://www.ocregister.com/2012/05/17/death-march-survivor-finally-tells-story/

The Big Picture. United States Army. *Battle of Manila*. 1950-63. https://www.youtube.com/watch?v=j3l6d_o1mxc&t=439s

Budge, Kent G. "Philippine Islands." *The Pacific War Online Wikipedia*. Last Modified 2013. Last Accessed August 4, 2017. http://pwencycl.kgbudge.com/P/h/Philippine_Islands.htm

Burgess, Val. "Billibid Prison." *Wars' Voices Are you Listening?*. Last Modified July 12, 2014. Last Accessed August 3, 2017. http://www.warsvoices.org/location/bilibid-prison/

Burgess, Val. "Santa Tomas Camp." *Wars' Voices Are you Listening?*. Last Modified August 1, 2014. Last Accessed August 3, 2017. http://www.warsvoices.org/location/santa-tomas-manilla-luzon/

Calugas Jr., Jose. "Jose C. Calugas Sr." *US-Japan Dialogue on POWs*. Last Accessed August 3rd 2017. http://www.us-japandialogueonpows.org/Calugas.htm http://www.historylink.org/File/10939

Chun, Clayton. *The Fall of the Philippines 1941-1942*. Great Britain: Osprey Publishing, 2012.

Costello, John. *The Pacific War 1941-1945*. Atlantic Communications, 1981.

Department of National Defense Philippine Veterans Affairs Office. *Legacy of Heroes: The Story of Bataan and Corregidor*. Directed by Butch Nolasco. https://www.youtube.com/watch?v=ennb2ihsTR8

Diephof, Laureen. "Lorenzo Apilado, 100, Defied the Death March and Malaria," *The Californian*. Last Modified August 3, 2017. Last Accessed August 3, 2017. http://www.thecalifornian.com/story/life/2017/08/04/lorenzo-apilado-defied-bataan-death-march-malaria/104276172/

"An Evaluative Research in the Implementation of Assistance to Lolas of Crisis (ALCS) Project." *Department of Social Welfare and Devel-*

opment and the Asian Women's Fund. Last accessed August 2, 2017. http://www.awf.or.jp/pdf/ALCS.pdf

Gladwin, Lee A. "American POWs on Japanese Ships Take a Voyage into Hell," *U.S. National Archives and Records Administration, Prologue Magazine Vol. 35, No. 4* (Winter 2003). Last modified July 19, 2017. Last Accessed August 3, 2017. https://www.archives.gov/publications/prologue/2003/winter/hell-ships-1.html

GOVPH. "BRIEFER: Massacres in the Battle of Manila." *Philippine Presidential Museum & Library*, Last Accessed July 30th, 2017. http://malacanang.gov.ph/75083-briefer-massacres-in-the-battle-of-manila/.

History Channel. *Rescue at Dawn: The Los Banos raid*. 2004. https://www.youtube.com/watch?v=ppH0JLaThEE

History Channel. *Shootout: Raid on Bataan Death Camp*. Directed by Louis C. Tarantino. 2006. https://www.youtube.com/watch?v=YY9V-7vPK5-8.

"Jesus Villamor: Soldier, Spy." *Filipinas Heritage Library*. Last Accessed August 3rd, 2017. http://www.filipinaslibrary.org.ph/filipiniana-library/filipiniana/70-features/267-jesus-villamor

Li, Peter. *The Search for Justice: Japanese War Crimes*. New Brunswick: Transaction Publishers, 2003.

Llorente, Bev. "Bataan Death March Survivor Recalls Terrifying Experience." *ABS-CBN News*. Last Modified December 7, 2016. Last Accessed July 31, 2017. https://www.balitangamerica.tv/bataan-death-march-survivor-recalls-terrifying-experience/

McCall-Washington, Ashley N. "Surrender at Bataan Led to One of the Worst Atrocities in Modern Warfare," *USO*. Last Modified November 14th, 2015. Last Accessed August 3rd, 2017. https://www.uso.org/stories/122-surrender-at-bataan-led-to-one-of-the-worst-atrocities-in-modern-warfare.

CHECK OUT ALL OF OUR PUBLICATION ON PACIFIC ASIA WAR

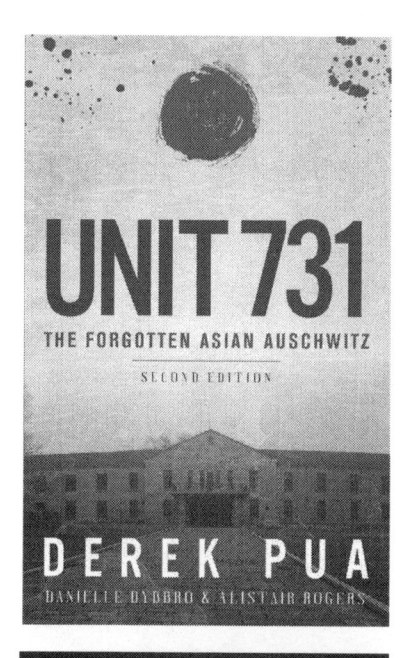

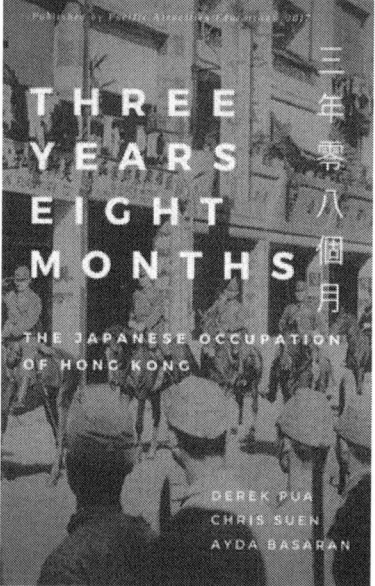

Made in the USA
Monee, IL
05 July 2024